THE
BIKER
IN THE
MIDWEST

D1296193

Best Bike Rides Series

THE BEST BIKE RIDES IN THE MIDWEST

Illinois · Indiana · Iowa · Michigan Minnesota · Ohio · Wisconsin

SECOND EDITION

by

Phil Van Valkenberg

A Voyager Book

The Globe Pequot Press

Old Saybrook, Connecticut

Photo credits: pp. viii, 83: courtesy Apple Cider Century; p. 11: by Carolyn Prieb/Chicagoland Bicycle Federation

Cover photo by Tony Demin/Westlight

Library of Congress Cataloging-in-Publication Data

Van Valkenberg, Phil, 1945–
  The best bike rides in the Midwest: Illinois, Indiana, Iowa, Michigan, Minnesota, Ohio, Wisconsin / by Phil Van Valkenberg. — 2nd ed.
      p.   cm. — (Best bike rides series)
"A Voyager book."
  ISBN 0–7627–0050–5 (recycled paper)
  1. Bicycle touring—Middle West—Guidebooks. 2. Middle West—Guidebooks. I. Title. II. Series
  GV1045.5.M55V36 1997
  796.6'4'0977—dc21
                                                                    97-12106
                                                                    CIP

♻ This book is printed on recycled paper.
Manufactured in the United States of America
Second Edition/First Printing

For Lily Marie

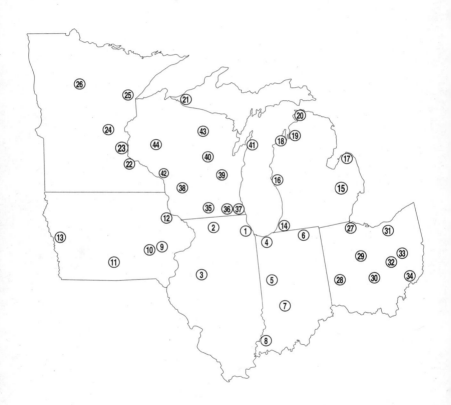

Contents

Introduction

When you think of the Midwest, you probably picture quiet roads, dairy farms, blue lakes, and rivers winding through green woods and gentle hills and past small towns. If you live here, you know that this combination makes the area one of the finest places in the country for bicycle touring.

Take a look at the bicycling adventures you'll find in the Midwest:

- On the "Amishland Ramble" in Indiana, you can trade pace with horse-drawn Amish buggies and visit stores where the "plain people" display the handiwork that is the product of their unmechanized lifestyle.
- In Michigan the "Cherry Blossom Cruise" will lead you over rolling hills carpeted with fragrant pink orchards in full bloom.
- Riding the "Lake Pepin Challenge," you'll cruise beneath towering limestone bluffs on the Minnesota and Wisconsin banks of the mighty Mississippi.
- In Ohio you can experience the beauty and romance of days past on the "Covered Bridge Ramble" in an area that has the country's largest concentration of these lovely structures.
- On the "Ride for Nature Ramble," you'll explore the Midwest's equivalent of New England's coastline as you pedal from the Wisconsin shoreline of Lake Michigan to a picturesque village on Green Bay.
- You can pause to step from rock to rock across the Mississippi River at its source deep in the virgin pine forest of northern Minnesota on the "Headwaters Challenge."
- The wide green boulevards of the nation's second largest city and the shadows of America's tallest buildings are on the route when you ride the "Chicago Boulevard Lakefront Ramble."
- You can cruise along the country's first transcontinental highway, now a quiet, forgotten Iowa back road, on the "Lincoln Highway Challenge."

The Midwest's rural roadway system was designed to serve farmers and tourists, but it's also ideal for bicycling. Back roads make up a scenic, lightly traveled network of paved routes that connect little towns. The small communities that offer services for visitors and farmers are also part of the appeal of touring in the Midwest. They are often a window to America's past, places where progress hasn't erased or overwhelmed the efforts of our forebears. The solid architecture of the last century sits proudly on every Main Street.

Small-town lifestyles can contribute to a memorable tour as well. In this slower-paced world, people gather at local cafes, and they'll want to know where you've been and where you're going. A meal at a small-town restaurant will have some character that distinguishes your visit from just another stop at a fast-food franchise. Country stores and other mom-and-pop enterprises often dot the countryside and offer a chance to pick up supplies and meet the locals. Staying at resorts, inns, or bed-and-breakfast homes gives you a chance to get to know an area even better.

Native American culture and history can often be found in the Midwest, for here a wide variety of cultures flourished from the end of the last glacial epoch to historic times. Moundbuilders left massive reminders of thriving cultures that belie the Hollywood image of Indians. Conflicts between encroaching settlers in the Midwest played out a chapter of our history that determined the ultimate shape of the nation. Native Americans remain a part of the culture of the Midwest today, controlling their destiny on reservations that are nations within this nation.

The scenery and terrain of the Midwest make for wonderful bicycling experiences. Woods and woodlots abound between neat farmsteads, and they shelter winged and four-legged forest creatures that are best spotted from a quietly approaching bicycle.

When it comes to lakes and waterways, the Midwest is unequaled. The Great Lakes are America's inland seas. Their vast expanses hold the largest store of fresh water in the world, and their depths are the resting place of more shipwrecks than anywhere else in the nation. Bays with lighthouses, maritime lore, and restaurants serving fresh fish are part of any tour along the lakeshore.

The Mississippi, America's greatest river, begins in the deep woods of northern Minnesota and winds down past towering limestone bluffs along the Wisconsin, Iowa, and Illinois shores. The Ohio River forms the southern boundary for the region covered here. Tributaries to both mighty rivers are the scenic setting for many of these tours.

We don't have any true mountains in the Midwest, but the terrain here is seldom really flat. For the most part it rolls in a way that makes cycling interesting but not humbling. Instead of being exhausted, you'll feel exhilarated topping most Midwest hills. Land like this invites variety. You'll seldom find mile upon mile of the same scenery.

The tours presented between these covers are fine examples of the Midwest bicycling experience. They were chosen mainly from routes included in annual rides organized by local bicycle clubs. Some rides have been held for twenty years or more, and others are relatively new. They may attract thousands of riders or just a few score. Tours range in length from 24 to more than 100 miles. You can use this guide to ride the tour on your own or choose to join other cyclists on the day of the organized ride. Either way you're in for some great cycling in America's heartland.

Safety, Planning, and Efficiency: The Keys to a Great Tour

A safe bike trip is a happy bike trip, and the number-one aspect that makes it so is a safety-first attitude. I'll give you tips that will help you achieve that goal, but, ultimately, it's up to you to make safety the top priority. The preparations you make before you leave are also part of the mix of a tour with happy memories. There's more to it than just dragging the old bike out of the garage. Efficient riding technique will carry you farther and faster on the power your body is capable of producing. Your riding style and the fit of frame, seat, and handlebars can make the difference between pleasure and pain.

Practice safety full-time. A bicycle is recognized as a vehicle with the legal right to use the roadway except where specifically prohibited. You have the obligation to obey all of the normal rules of the road, plus a few more specific to bicycling.

- Ride on the right side of the roadway.
- Use hand signals to indicate turns to other riders and motor vehicles.

In Michigan you are required to ride on a bicycle side path when it parallels the road. I don't believe there are any routes in this book where this requirement applies.

Beyond the law there are many bicycling skills and habits that might be called cycling common sense and are important ingredients in a safe tour.

- **Be seen!** Wear brightly colored clothing. It will make both oncoming and overtaking motorists aware of your presence sooner.
- **Ride straight.** It sounds simple, but it takes practice. See how long you can stay on the white line on the right side of the road. You needn't ride it for miles, but if you can't stay on it for 50 yards, you're probably zigzagging down the road and creating a hazard to yourself, other cyclists, and motorists. Riding with slightly flexed elbows will help. This keeps normal body movement from affecting the steering.
- **Be aware of all traffic, front, side, and back.** It's easy to lull yourself into a sense of security on a quiet road, but you must always remember that you're sharing it with motor vehicles. As you approach intersections, make sure that crossing motorists have made eye contact with you even if you have the right of way. Check over your shoulder for overtaking traffic when turning or moving to the left to avoid a road hazard. Practice this check so you can do it without swerving. Helmet, eyeglass, or bicycle-mounted rear-view mirrors can serve this function, but if they are not properly designed, mounted, or adjusted, they can give a false sense of security that can spell disaster. Sound offers a warning of overtaking cars, but don't rely on it alone; use your eyes.
- **Apply your brakes with care.** Use the brakes to slow your speed before you get into a hazardous situation. Tight, blind downhill corners should be approached with caution. Any hazard such as potholes or wet leaves is best approached at slow speeds.
- **Load your bike properly.** A wide assortment of racks and bags

are available to carry various amounts of cargo. Divide up the load so it is distributed as evenly as possible and carried as low as possible if large amounts such as camping gear are being carried. Never strap a loose, flapping jacket to the handlebars or rear rack; it can easily get caught in spinning spokes—with terrible results.

- **Wear a good bike helmet.** Helmet design has made great strides in the past few years. Today helmets are light, well ventilated, and inexpensive. Buy one that fits you well and has a strap system that can be adjusted for comfort and security. Look inside the helmet for an approval sticker from one of several testing organizations. I don't know of any unapproved models on the market today, but in the past some helmets were not much better protection than the box they came in.
- **Use extra caution crossing railroad tracks and other road hazards.** I've tried to identify poor railroad crossings on the routes in this book, but any crossing should be treated with care. Crossings are often in poor repair, and they were never designed with bicycling in mind. The worst ones cross the road at an acute angle. You should slow as you approach and, checking for overtaking traffic, swing out and try to cross as perpendicular as possible. In the areas populated by the Amish, be careful of ruts left in the pavement by their narrow buggy wheels. These ruts can catch a bike tire and cause a spill.
- **Look out for dogs and other animals that may run in the road.** Dogs should be controlled by their owners and stay on their property. If they do pursue you on the roadway or threaten to, use stern commands like "Stay" and "Go home." If this fails to halt the attack, slow your bike, dismount, and walk away with the bike between you and the dog. Be careful of motorized traffic in this situation. Stopping usually ends the excitement of the chase. Report attacks to the local sheriff's office. Dogs and other animals should always be treated with caution because they can easily decide to run across your path at the last second.
- **Make sure your equipment fits and is in good repair.** A poorly fitted bike can cause fatigue that brings on inattention and carelessness. Faulty components can also lead to accidents. Brakes, spokes, gear systems, and bearings must all be well ad-

justed, and tires have to be in excellent shape. The light weight of the modern bike won't allow much abuse or perform well when everything isn't 100 percent. If you aren't competent to keep your bike in top shape, take it to a bike shop with good mechanics. It's well worth the cost.

A Few Creature Comforts Go a Long Way

- **Ride a frame that fits you right.** As a rule of thumb, you should be able to stand over the top tube of the bike with between 1 and 2 inches of clearance and be able to touch the handlebar with the tip of your fingers when you place your elbow on the tip of the saddle. While off-the-shop-floor bikes come in different frame sizes, most are designed for people of average build. If you're long or short in trunk, arms, or legs, you may need a custom fit. Today many shops have devices for measuring a precise fit.
- **Adjust your saddle correctly.** Your knee should be slightly bent when you place your heel on the pedal at the bottom of the crank rotation. A saddle that's too high or too low can cause knee problems.
- **Wear appropriate clothing.** Bike shorts, shoes, eyewear, gloves, tights, jerseys, and windbreakers are all designed to make bicycling more pleasurable and efficient. On a long ride a flapping jacket or baggy sweatpants will slow you down, and an unpadded crotch seam can rub you raw. Bicycle clothing is often stylish, well made, and suitable for other recreation as well. Dress in layers if the weather is less than ideal and you'll be comfortable and look proficient as you ride.

Train to Avoid Strain

- **Gear up for bike touring by easing into it.** Bicycling is an ideal life-sport that is about as low-impact as you can get. Beyond the aesthetics of cycling, there are great benefits to be had for the cardiovascular system. Bike touring falls on the endurance end of the cycling scale, and preparation is important. Ride frequently—three or four times per week—until you can comfortably handle a distance at least half the length of the tour you plan to ride. Choose short tours early in the year, and leave the longer ones for later, when you're more fit.

- **Polish your pedaling technique.** Many people turn the pedals too slowly and with an uneven motion when seated. When you learned to ride as a child, someone probably told you to push down on the pedals, and you may still be riding that way today. You're most efficient when you rotate the pedals, applying pressure as evenly as possible through all 360 degrees. Turning the pedals at between sixty and ninety revolutions per minute is also recommended for efficiency, with greater benefit toward the higher end of the range if you're conditioned to that speed. Toe clips and/or new clipless shoe and pedal systems now available for touring are indispensable in achieving these goals. They allow you to pull up on the backstroke and get the most out of your muscle mass.
- **Use your whole body when climbing.** Most climbing should be done in the saddle. Place your hands on the straight part of the handlebars near the stem and slide back on the saddle. This allows you to get more of a forward push on the pedals and use your calf and back muscles more effectively. For accelerating on short climbs or for a break on long climbs, you can get out of the saddle. This was called "pumping" when I was a kid, but it uses a lot of energy and needs to be done efficiently for endurance riding. Grip the handlebars near the brake levers on recurve bars or near the end or on the extensions on mountain-bike bars. Use your upper body to pull up on the handlebar as you push down on the pedal on the same side. At the same time pull up on the opposite side. This produces a side-to-side rocking motion with the bike, and your revolutions per minute will slow by about twenty to thirty revolutions below your normal seated spin.
- **Take it easy.** A tour is not a race, but even if it were, you'd be better off riding with your elbows and shoulders relaxed. Pedal

at a comfortable pace well below your maximum. This will ensure that your energy will carry you through to the finish.

• **Ride with others.** Joining a bike club is a smart move. You can learn a lot about bicycling by riding with more experienced cyclists. The extra effort needed to keep up on training rides will pay off in better conditioning. On a tour, however, ride at your own pace, and don't burn out trying to keep up. If it's a social tour, the stronger riders should slow down or wait for you; don't forget your obligation to friends if you are the strong rider. There are certain guidelines for riding in a tight group. Riding straight is number one. Don't brake sharply without warning. If you have to stop, call out or hold one arm down if riders are behind you. Call out or point out hazards in the road. If you're at the front, call out "Car up" if you see an oncoming vehicle, or if you're at the back, call out "Car back" when one is overtaking. If you're one of the strong riders in a group, take turns with others "pulling" at the front. This divides the work of pushing into the wind for the rest of the group. Never overlap your front wheel with the rear wheel of the bike in front of you.

How to Use This Book

Each of the tours in *The Best Bike Rides in the Midwest* is placed into one of four categories to help define its level of difficulty.

• **Rambles** are the easiest. The distances will be less than 35 miles, and you won't find extreme climbs along the routes. These are ideal for early season rides or for novices. Don't forget to train, though; these tours are not just a ride around the park.

• **Cruises** begin to dice things up a bit. They'll always be less than 70 miles and more than 30 miles. This range encompasses the popular "metric century" category of rides that are 100 kilometers, or 62 miles, in length. A cruise of this distance will be predominantly flat. A short cruise, on the other hand, could have a good climb along the route.

• **Challenges** get serious. The distances will range from around 45 to 80 miles, and the terrain may be where the challenge comes in. Rides with little relief from a strong prevailing wind also fit this category.

• **Classics** are crowning achievements in bike touring. A ride of this class may be the goal of a season of preparation or another notch on the handlebar for the extremely fit. Expect distances from around 80 miles to more than 110 miles, with climbs that may be numerous, steep, and long.

Some of the rides, particularly longer ones, offer shorter options that allow you to enjoy the area without taking on the long miles or serve as bailouts if you bit off more than you could chew. All of the ratings are guidelines, and your choice should be based on the best assessment of your preparation you can make. Also, a tour that's an easy cruise on one day can be a challenge on another if the weather is adverse.

Use the maps in conjunction with the cue sheets that provide specific directions at each turn. A bicycle computer is indispensable for following a cue sheet. Be sure to turn it off if you have to leave the route and on again when you return. It isn't possible to make the maps detailed enough to name or show every road or street with this format, so following the cues is extremely important.

Note the availability of food along the route you've chosen. The Midwest is a great place for on-route munchies, with cafes, country stores, and taverns in abundance. But on some routes you may have long stretches where you'll have to rely on the energy food and drink that you've carried along.

Disclaimer

The Globe Pequot Press assumes no liability for accidents happening to, or injuries sustained by, readers who engage in the activities described in this book.

Illinois

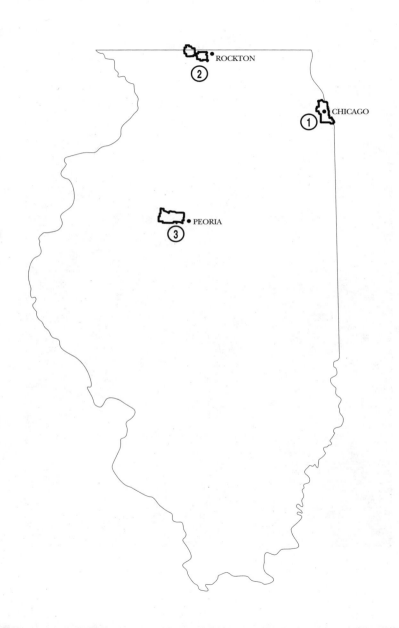

Illinois

1

Chicago Boulevard Lakefront Ramble

A bike tour in downtown Chicago? You must be crazy! A reasonable reaction if you've ever been in the Windy City on a weekday. But on a Sunday morning, Chicago is a different place. This is the time to bike one of the world's great cities, an unmatched collection of impressive buildings, green boulevards, and parks. The Chicagoland Bicycle Federation organizes the tour, *Chicagoland* being defined as a political amusement park by Director Randy Neufeld. On the third Sunday of each June, nearly 5,000 riders cover the route.

Chicago's architectural reputation is owed in part to the Great Chicago Fire of 1871. It spurred a building boom that attracted brilliant and innovative architects and set a tradition of civic pride that continues to this day. After the fire a circuit of boulevards connecting parks, neighborhoods, and businesses was built. An 8-mile-an-hour speed limit was set for buggies and bicycles to ensure a relaxing ride. Today remember that you're riding in an urban environment with motorized traffic. Be careful, but when the traffic is light it's easy to enjoy the greenery, architecture, and sculpture at bicycle speeds.

The tour starts at the University of Chicago, the site of the 1893 Columbian Exposition, the first great world's fair. The fair's amusements were on Midway Plaisance, and carnival attractions have been called midways ever since. The route follows the boulevards that once formed the southern, western, and northern boundaries of the city.

As you head south along the route into the downtown area known as the Loop, you'll ride through a living museum of urban architecture. On the east side of LaSalle Street, just over the Chicago

River, you'll pass one of the newest additions, the controversial State of Illinois Building. Known as the "Blue Beast," the Helmut Jahn–designed, steel-and-glass structure was built in 1985. Inadvertently, it became a giant solar-collector, and employees couldn't stand the heat on sunny days.

At 20 North LaSalle you'll pass the old Chicago Stock Exchange, designed by skyscraper pioneer Louis Sullivan. The exterior decoration of the 1895 building is characteristic of Sullivan and shows the influence on his employee Frank Lloyd Wright. The world's tallest building, the Skidmore, Owens, and Merrill–designed Sears Tower, is visible west of the route as you near Jackson Drive.

The Rookery Building, at 209 South LaSalle, was designed by the firm of Burnham and Root in 1886. It pioneered the iron-skeleton frame construction that made modern skyscrapers possible. Frank Lloyd Wright designed the ground-story court. The same firm designed the sixteen-story Monadnock Building, at 53 West Jackson Drive, in 1891. With walls 6 feet thick at the base, it was as high as traditional masonry-supported wall construction could go.

The Chicago Fire may have inspired an architectural boom, but the Flood of 1992 helped revive bicycling. When the Chicago River burst into underground tunnels and closed down the economic heart of mid-America, on-street parking in the Loop was restricted, making biking easier. Now the Chicagoland Bicycle Federation has worked with the city to place 2,500 parking racks to make it even more bicycle-friendly.

Back at the tour starting point, take a short side trip north to 5757 South Woodlawn Avenue to see the Robie House. Built in 1909, it's the epitome of Frank Lloyd Wright's prairie-style architecture.

The Basics

Start: Park on the street on the Midway Plaisance at the University of Chicago, and start in front of Ida Noyes Hall.
Length: 34.8 miles.
Terrain: Very flat.

Food: There are opportunities too numerous to mention along the route; however, at the corner of Clyborn and Webster and to the east on Webster you'll find a number of interesting cafes and restaurants.

For more information: Chicago Boulevard Lakefront Tour, Chicago Bicycle Federation, 417 Dearborn St., Suite 1800, Chicago, IL 60605; (312) 42–PEDAL, e-mail: chibikefed@aol.com. Chicago Convention & Tourism Bureau, McCormick Place On-The-Lake, Chicago, IL 60616; (312) 567–8500; Web site: http://www. chicago.il.org.

Bicycle service: Many locations in Chicago.

Miles & Directions

- 0.0 Proceed west on Midway Plaisance (59th St.).
- 0.5 Straight on Payne Dr., which becomes Morgan Dr., which becomes Garfield Blvd.
- 4.9 Right on Western Blvd.
- 8.5 Left on 26th St.
- 9.0 Right on California Blvd.
- 9.2 Left on 24th Blvd.
- 9.5 Right on Marshall Blvd., which becomes Sacramento Dr.
- 10.5 Left on Douglas Blvd.
- 11.4 Right on Independence Blvd.
- 12.6 Right on Washington Blvd.
- 12.8 Left on Central Park Dr. through Garfield Park.
- 13.4 Right on Franklin Blvd.
- 14.2 Left on Sacramento Blvd., which becomes Humbolt Blvd.
- 16.4 Right on Palmer Blvd., following it around Palmer Square.
- 16.8 Right on Kedzie Blvd.
- 17.2 Right on Logan Blvd.
- 18.7 Right on Diversey Pkwy.
- 19.0 Right on Clyborn Ave.
- 20.1 Left on Webster Ave.
- 21.2 Right on Lincoln Ave.
- 21.9 Right on Wells St.

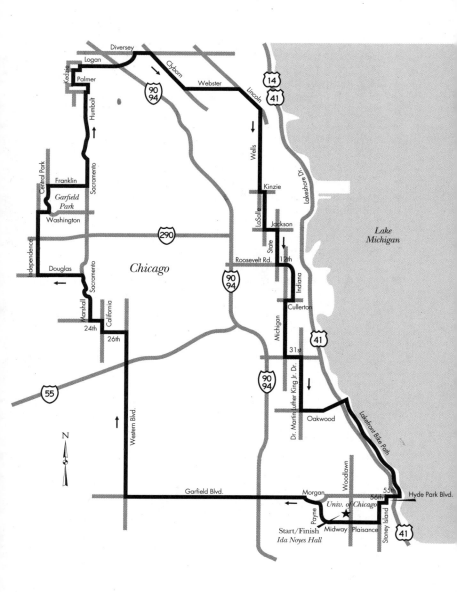

- 23.6 Left on Kinzie St.
- 23.7 Right on LaSalle St.
- 24.6 Left on Jackson Blvd.
- 24.9 Right on State St.
- 25.7 Left on 12th St. opposite Roosevelt Rd.
- 25.9 Right on Indiana St.
- 26.7 Right on Cullerton St.
- 26.8 Left on Michigan Ave.
- 28.1 Left on 31st St.
- 28.5 Right on Dr. Martin Luther King Jr. Dr.
- 29.6 Left on Oakwood Blvd.
- 30.5 Right on Lakefront Bike Path.
- 33.0 Right on 55th St.
- 33.4 Left on Hyde Park Blvd.
- 33.5 Right on 56th St.
- 33.7 Left on Stoney Island.
- 34.2 Right on Midway Plaisance.
- 34.8 Arrive at Ida Noyes Hall at Woodlawn Ave.

2

Blackhawk Metric Challenge

Black Hawk and the Black Hawk War are at the core of the history of this part of the Midwest. Black Hawk was in his sixties when he led a contingent of Sauk and Fox people across the Mississippi and up the Rock River to reclaim lands they'd been cheated of. They were called the British Band because Black Hawk fought for the English in the War of 1812. Twenty years later he was told that the British in Canada would help him drive the Americans out. Just south of Rockford he learned that the information was false.

Black Hawk decided to return to Iowa, but at the same time his band was attacked by the Illinois Militia, who were badly routed in the fight. There was no turning back then. He continued up the Rock River and to the eventual destruction of his people by the U.S. Army. Black Hawk was captured and paraded through the East. When he met with President Jackson, he told him, "I took up the hatchet to revenge injuries my people could no longer endure." The war made this region of the Midwest famous and brought a flood of settlers. Ironically, both Abraham Lincoln and Jefferson Davis served in the war.

Black Hawk's name appears often in the Rockford area, and he is respected for his bravery. The Blackhawk Bicycle Club created this tour in 1977, and it has been a popular Memorial Day Weekend event ever since. The tour begins on the banks of the Rock River and explores rolling hills and river bottomland of the Sugar, Otter, Raccoon, and Pecatonica that would have been familiar to Black Hawk.

Heading east from River Road, the route rolls along the ridges and valleys that would have been prairie in Black Hawk's day. As you turn north, you'll have a nice roll into the broad valley where the Pecatonica joins the Sugar River.

Continuing east you'll find the village of Durand, a typical midwestern farm community. As you head north, you'll follow Otter Creek before a long, gradual climb up Laona Ridge. The roll off the top includes a great view of the Sugar River Valley. The village of Avon is an example of how sad rural America can get, but even junkyards have some character.

As you turn south and east, you'll once again dive into the river valleys and grind your way out on your way to Rockton, the last town on the route. You'll find it a quaint, small river town with restaurants and ice cream stands well worth the visit.

The Basics

Start: Atwood Homestead Forest Preserve, 8900 Old River Rd., off Hwy. 2, north of the city of Rockford.
Length: 34.7 or 60.9 miles.
Terrain: Rolling to moderately hilly.
Food: You'll find a grocery store and soft drink machine in Harrison and a soft drink machine by the post office in Shirland. In Durand you'll find a restaurant with a big cow statue, a grocery, and an ice cream stand. In Rockton are an ice cream stand, a grocery, and restaurants.
For more information: Blackhawk Bicycle and Ski Club, P.O. Box 6443, Rockford, IL 61125; Arland Brass; (815) 814–7208. Rockford Area Chamber of Commerce, 515 N. Court, Rockford, IL 61125; (815) 987–8100.
Bicycle service: In Rockford.

Miles & Directions

- 0.0 From the parking area in Atwood Homestead Forest Preserve, proceed south on Atwood Park Rd.
- 1.4 Right on Old River Rd.
- 2.2 Left on Gleasman Rd.
- 5.1 Left on Owen Center Rd.

- 5.5 Right on Steward Rd.
- 7.1 Right on Clark Rd.
- 8.1 Left on Favor Rd.
- 9.4 Right on Meridian Rd.
- 9.6 Left on Wishop Rd.
- 10.6 Right on Harrison Rd.
- 12.1 Left on Rte. 75 in Harrison, where you'll find a grocery store and soft drink machine.
- 12.2 Right on Shirland Rd., along Sugar River.
- 14.4 Left on Winslow Rd. in Shirland, where you'll find a soft drink machine by the post office.

To complete the shorter 34.7-mile route, turn right on Hauley Rd. at mile 15.8. At mile 17.1 at Forest Preserve Rd., turn right and pick up the directions below at mile 43.2.

- 17.6 Right on Fritz Rd.
- 19.6 Left on Wheeler Rd.
- 19.7 Right on Fritz Rd.
- 21.1 Right on Rte. 70 in the town of Durand, where you'll find a restaurant with a big cow statue, a grocery, and an ice cream stand.
- 21.3 Left on W. Main St., which becomes Durand Rd.
- 21.8 Right on Patterson Rd.
- 23.1 Left on Rock Grove Rd.
- 24.6 Right on Anderson Rd.
- 27.5 At the Illinois-Wisconsin state line at State Line Rd., Anderson Rd. becomes Green County T.
- 29.3 Straight onto Douglas Rd. at the Rock County line, where County T turns left.
- 30.5 Left on Hopkins Rd.
- 31.9 Right on Beloit-Newark Rd.
- 33.0 Proceed straight through the village of Avon.
- 34.2 Right on Nelson Rd.
- 34.9 Left on Carroll Rd. (scenic views of wildlife area).
- 36.8 Right on Brandherm Rd.
- 39.7 Right on Rock County K (Roy Rd.).

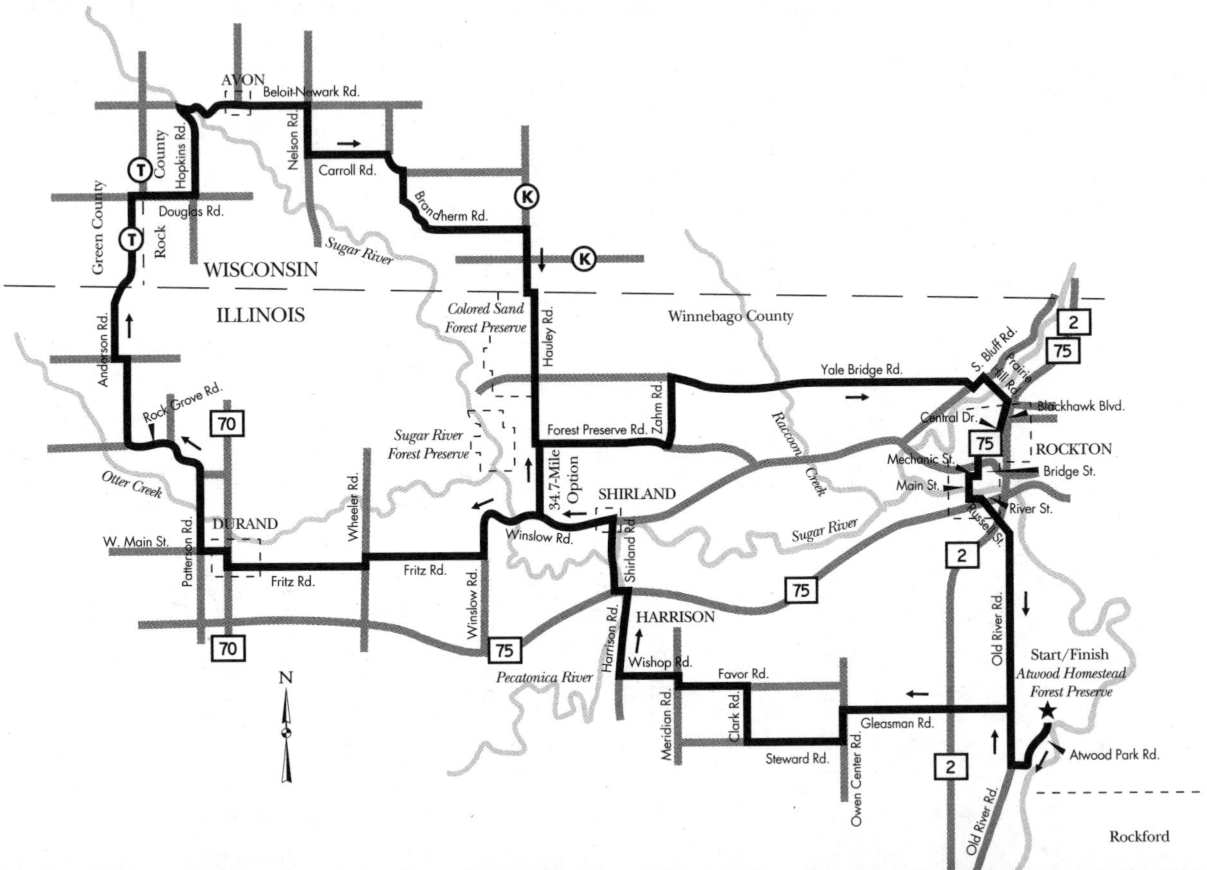

AVON
Beloit-Newark Rd.
Nelson Rd.
Carroll Rd.
Brandherm Rd.
K
K
County
Hopkins Rd.
T
T
Green County
Rock
Douglas Rd.
Sugar River
WISCONSIN
ILLINOIS
Anderson Rd.
Colored Sand Forest Preserve
Hauley Rd.
Winnebago County
Yale Bridge Rd.
S. Bluff Rd.
Prairie Hill Rd.
2
75
Blackhawk Blvd.
Central Dr.
75
ROCKTON
Bridge St.
Mechanic St.
Main St.
River St.
Russell St.
Rock Grove Rd.
70
Zahm Rd.
Forest Preserve Rd.
Raccoon Creek
Sugar River Forest Preserve
Otter Creek
34.7-Mile Option
SHIRLAND
Sugar River
DURAND
W. Main St.
Patterson Rd.
Wheeler Rd.
Winslow Rd.
Shirland Rd.
2
Fritz Rd.
Fritz Rd.
75
Winslow Rd.
Harrison Rd.
HARRISON
Old River Rd.
70
75
Wishop Rd.
Pecatonica River
Favor Rd.
Start/Finish
Atwood Homestead Forest Preserve
N
Meridian Rd.
Clark Rd.
Gleasman Rd.
Steward Rd.
Owen Center Rd.
2
Atwood Park Rd.
Old River Rd.
Rockford

- 40.2 Straight onto Hauley Rd. where County K turns left.
- 43.2 Left on Forest Preserve Rd.
- 45.5 Left on Zahm Rd.
- 46.6 Right on Yale Bridge Rd.
- 51.9 Left on S. Bluff Rd.
- 52.1 Right on Prairie Hill Rd.; cross the Rock River Bridge.
- 52.6 Right on Blackhawk Blvd.
- 53.1 Left on Central Dr.
- 53.2 Right on Rte. 75 in the town of Rockton, where you'll find an ice cream stand, a grocery, and restaurants.
- 53.6 Left on Bridge St.
- 54.0 Right on Mechanic St.
- 54.2 Left on Main St.; cross the Rock River Bridge.
- 54.5 Left on River St.
- 54.8 Right on Russell St., which becomes Old River Rd.
- 59.5 Left on Atwood Park Rd.
- 60.9 Arrive at Atwood Homestead Forest Preserve parking area.

3

No Baloney Cruise

Most people think that central Illinois is flat, and, if you've driven past mile upon mile of cornfields where the highest point on the horizon is a grain elevator, you might be convinced it's true. But there are places, like the twisting valleys that feed into the Illinois River near Peoria, where the land assumes a different character. It's in this country that the Illinois Valley Wheelmen run their annual No Baloney Ride on the first weekend of June. In addition to this route, the event includes 25-, 75-, and 100-mile options.

A ride name like "No Baloney" deserves some explanation. Actually, it's an assurance that there won't be any baloney sandwiches at the food stops. Why is this necessary? Because one year the ride food chairman stocked the stops with baloney sandwiches. Hungry cyclists spontaneously chanted "No baloney." Hence the ride name and more palatable food-stop fare.

Wildlife Prairie Park, where the ride begins, is a trip in itself. It's a living museum of pioneer life and native plants and animals that characterized the Illinois prairie. Herds of buffalo and elk can be viewed from an overlook a short walk from the visitor center. A 2-mile hike will take you past black bears, cougars, bobcats, wolves, coyotes, and foxes. There are also an authentic pioneer general store and a farmstead with oxen, horses, and goats that can be petted. A commissary serves a Sunday brunch or a daily hot special, as well as items from hot dogs to garden salads. The 2,000-acre park is partially on land reclaimed from strip mining.

Riding out of the park, you'll enjoy a steep roll 100 feet down into the valley of the west branch of Kickapoo Creek. You'll ride east in the valley long enough to warm up your legs for the moderate climbs that will take you north and west onto open farmland planted with corn and soybeans. It's back into the woods as you turn into Jubilee College State Park, site of an Episcopal seminary founded in 1840, one of the earliest colleges in Illinois. In the 7 miles from there to Brimfield you'll face ten hills, but all are manageable.

South of Brimfield you'll roll over land punctuated with scattered ponds left over from the days when the area was strip-mined for coal. Most of the visible scars from mining are now overgrown. Finally, there is one more run down into the valley of the Kickapoo before the steep climb back to the park.

The Basics

Start: Park at Wildlife Prairie Park (admission required), 3 miles south of I–74 on Edwards Rd. and Taylor Rd.
Length: 45.1 miles.
Terrain: Flat, rolling, and hilly.
Food: There is a restaurant at Wildlife Prairie Park. In Brimfield you'll find an ice cream shop/cafe, a convenience store, and taverns.
For more information: No Baloney, Illinois Valley Wheelmen, 1318 W. McQueen, Peoria, IL 61604; (309) 688–0922, e-mail: sjoslin@heartland.bradley.edu. Peoria Convention & Visitors Bureau, 403 N.E. Jefferson St., Peoria, IL 61603; (309) 676–0303 or (800) 747–0302.
Bicycle service: In Peoria.

Miles & Directions

- 0.0 Ride west out of Wildlife Prairie Park.
- 0.3 Right on Taylor Rd. **Caution: steep downhill.**
- 1.0 Right on Rte. 8 at the village of Edwards.
- 4.4 Left on Koerner Rd.
- 6.0 Right on County 47 (Charter Oak Rd.).
- 6.8 Left on Orange Prairie Rd. just before the freeway.
- 8.7 Right on U.S. Hwy. 150. **Caution: Significant traffic may be encountered.**
- 9.0 Left on Rte. 91.

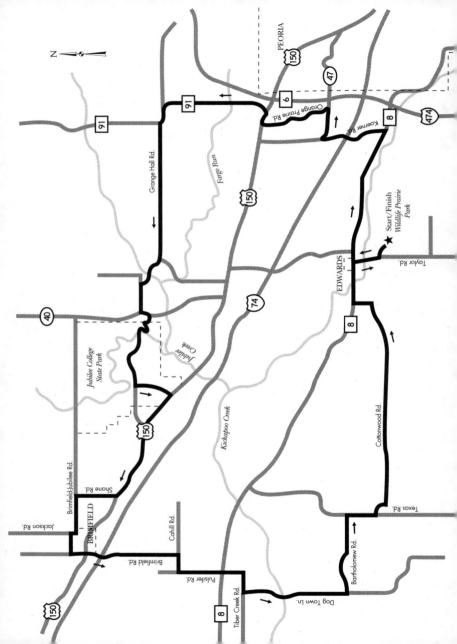

- 12.1 Left on Grange Hall Rd.
- 15.5 Bear right on Grange Hall Rd.
- 17.1 Left on County 40 (Princeville-Jubilee Rd.).
- 17.4 Right into Jubilee College State Park.
- 20.7 Right on U.S. Hwy. 150. **Caution: Significant traffic may be encountered.**
- 23.6 Right on Shane Rd.
- 24.7 Left on Brimfield-Jubilee Rd.
- 25.6 Right on Jackson Rd.
- 25.7 Left on Brimfield-Jubilee Rd.
- 26.3 Left on Brimfield Rd. into the town of Brimfield, where you'll find an ice cream shop/cafe, a convenience store, and taverns.
- 28.9 Right on Cahill Rd.
- 29.4 Left on Pulsifer Rd.
- 30.9 Right on Tiber Creek Rd.
- 31.4 Left on Dog Town Ln.
- 33.9 Left on Bartholomew Rd.
- 36.0 Right on Texas Rd.
- 36.7 Left on Cottonwood Rd.
- 42.7 Right on Rte. 8.
- 43.8 Right on Taylor Rd.
- 44.6 Left into Wildlife Prairie Park.
- 45.1 Arrive at parking lot.

Indiana

HOWE

⑥

CHESTERTON

④

⑤

BATTLE GROUND

BLOOMINGTON

⑦

⑧

DARMSTADT

Indiana

4

Lakeshore Cruise

The Indiana Dunes National Lakeshore is the destination of the annual Lakeshore Century. Held on the first Sunday after Labor Day, the tour offers four loops, ranging from 25 to 100 miles in length.

The dunes are the product of lake and wind. Lake Michigan defines the basin of a great glacial lobe of ice that pushed down from Canada. As it receded, about 14,000 years ago, the lake it left behind was much higher than it is today. The gradual dropping of the lake level created the series of parallel dune ridges that you'll ride over. Your first opportunity for a close look at a dune comes at the visitor center. A ten-minute slide show will explain some of the features you are about to see, and a short hike on the Calumet Dune Trail outside the center will give you a feel for the character of an inland dune.

As you ride north on E. State Park Road, you'll pass over the Tollston Dune and see the blue waters of Lake Michigan in the distance. A 1-mile hike on the Dune Ridge Trail will let you see the changing plant life that marks the dunes. Near the lake, the dunes are bare sand. Farther inland, grasses take hold, and, eventually, forest claims the dunes.

The dunes are a classroom case of how plants can adapt and in the process change the very environment around them. As grasses take hold, a little shade is provided that accommodates other plants. Decaying leaves and blades begin building up soil that allows trees to take root. Some plants, like the arctic bearberry and the northern jack pine, are remnants of the days when the glacier was melting nearby. Others that grow alongside them, like the prickly pear cactus, have moved in, finding a home in the sandy soil.

You'll reach the lakeshore at Kemil Beach, a great place to swim or relax after the ride. Heading east along Lake Front Drive, you'll pass the community of Beverly Shores. The unusual collection of homes built in the dunes has to do with the early promotion of the location. Homes displayed at the 1933 Chicago World's Fair were transported to Beverly Shores by barge to kick off the development.

Turning south and heading inland, you'll again cross the first two ridges of dunes before climbing the Glenwood Dune south of U.S. Highway 20. Though you won't be able to tell as you climb, this last dune gives way to the Lake Border Moraine. The moraines are parallel, jumbled bands of hills that mark the edge of the glacier's push. Like the dunes, the oldest moraines are farther from the lakeshore. The biggest moraine is the truly massive Valparaiso Moraine, which you'll ride over between Tratebas and Burdick roads. Expect 75- to 100-foot climbs and a good roll back toward the lakeshore.

The Basics

Start: Park at the Indiana Dunes National Lakeshore Visitor Center, just south of U.S. Hwy. 12 on Kemil Rd.
Length: 43.9 miles.
Terrain: Flat to rolling.
Food: In Chesterton there are a number of restaurants, bakeries, groceries, and convenience stores.
For more information: Calumet Crank Club, Inc., P.O. Box 1880, Valparaiso, IN 46384; (219) 766–2952. Porter County Convention, Recreation & Visitors Commission, 800 Indian Boundary Rd., Chesterton, IN 46304; (800) 283–TOUR. Indiana Dunes National Lakeshore, 1100 N. Mineral Springs Rd., Porter, IN 46304; (219) 926–7561.
Bicycle service: In Chesterton.

Miles & Directions

- 0.0 Ride north on County 300E (Kemil Rd.) from the Indiana Dunes National Lakeshore Visitor Center.

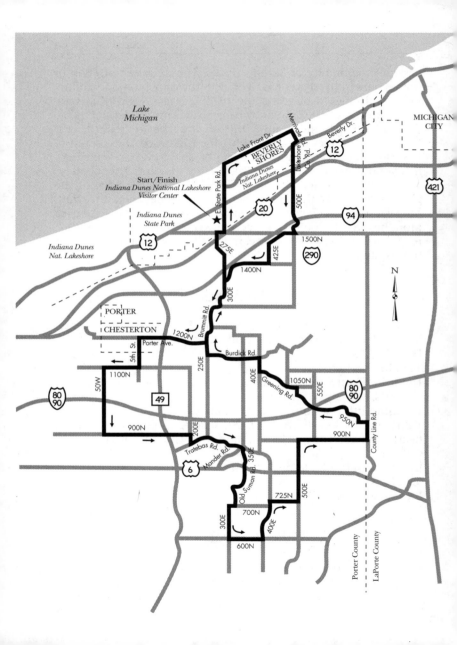

- 0.2 Straight across U.S. Hwy. 12 onto E. State Park Rd.
- 1.4 Right on Lake Front Dr.
- 3.6 Right on Merrivale Rd.
- 4.0 Right on Beverly Dr.
- 4.2 Left on Lakeshore Co. Rd.
- 5.0 Straight across U.S. Hwy. 12 onto County 500E.
- 5.4 Straight across U.S. Hwy. 20, staying on County 500E.
- 6.9 Right on County 1500N, which becomes County 425E as it turns south.
- 8.4 Right on County 1400N.
- 9.9 Left on County 300E, which becomes Brummitt Rd. and later County 250E.
- 11.9 Right on County 1200N, which becomes Porter Ave.
- 14.0 Left on 5th St. in the town of Chesterton, where you'll find restaurants, bakeries, groceries, and convenience stores.
- 14.9 Right on County 1100N.
- 15.9 Left on County 50W.
- 17.8 Left on County 900N.
- 20.2 Right on County 200E.
- 20.5 Left on Tratebas Rd.
- 21.9 Bear left on Tratebas Rd. at the junction with Mander Rd.
- 22.2 Right on County 350E.
- 22.9 Straight across U.S. Hwy. 6 onto Old Suman Rd.
- 24.2 Right on County 700N, which becomes County 300E as it turns south.
- 25.1 Left on County 600N.
- 26.1 Left on County 400E.
- 27.3 Right on County 725N.
- 28.1 Left on County 500E.
- 29.0 Straight across U.S. Hwy. 6 on County 500E.
- 30.0 Right on County 900N.
- 32.0 Left on County Line Rd.
- 32.6 Left on County 950N.
- 34.5 Right on County 550E.
- 34.7 Left on Greening Rd.
- 35.7 Left on Greening Rd. at the intersection with County 1050N.

- 36.8 Right on County 400E.
- 37.4 Left on Burdick Rd.
- 38.9 Right on County 250E.
- 39.7 Bear left on Brummitt Rd.
- 41.4 Bear left on County 300E, which becomes County 275E.
- 42.7 Straight across U.S. Hwy. 20 onto County 275E.
- 43.0 Right on County 1500N (Furnessville Rd.).
- 43.3 Left on County 300E (Kemil Rd.)
- 43.9 Arrive at Indiana Dunes National Lakeshore Visitor Center.

5

Wabash River Classic

"Tippecanoe and Tyler, Too" was the slogan that propelled William Henry Harrison into the presidency in 1841. It was a time in America when a reputation as an Indian fighter was excellent political fodder. Harrison's martial glory was forged thirty years before in a battle near the confluence of the Tippecanoe and Wabash rivers.

This ride begins at the Battlefield Interpretive Center, the site of the conflict between Harrison's soldiers and a union of tribes known as Tecumseh's Confederacy. First run in 1984, the bike ride is held the first Sunday in September and includes 40- and 60-mile routes as well as the century route.

The Wabash is the storied river of the state of Indiana. The sweet strains of the sentimental tune "Banks of the Wabash" are dear to every Indiana heart. But a bicycle tour along the Wabash is more than a ramble along a picturesque river; it's a lesson in the early history of the nation.

After the American Revolution the former colonists poured west over the Allegheny Mountains. Two Shawnee brothers, Tecumseh and Tenskwatawa, encouraged neighboring tribes to halt the expansion. Tenskwatawa, usually called the Prophet, urged his followers to abandon white influences, particularly alcohol. Harrison challenged him to prove his power by some awesome act like making the sun stand still. The Prophet called the tribes to him. As they watched in amazement, the light dimmed in a total eclipse of the sun. Some say the British tipped him off, but he had no trouble attracting warriors to his new village at Tippecanoe.

They had every right to settle in Indiana, but Harrison feared the intentions of the large union of sober, militant Indians. In November 1811, while Tecumseh was away, he marched on the village to demand surrender. The Prophet put him off for a day and secretly planned a predawn attack on Harrison's camp. The Indians were repulsed, and they soon deserted the Prophet, who had made a promise he couldn't keep. He'd told them they'd be invulnerable to the Long Knives' bullets.

Tecumseh returned to find his confederacy in a shambles, but he led his tribe to side with the British in the War of 1812. He won a number of early victories but was killed when the tide turned in 1813. Harrison rode his fame to the White House; he died a month after assuming office.

The Battleground Interpretive Center details the conflict of cultures that bloodied the Indiana ground. Riding out on Prophets Rock Road, you'll pass the large stone that, legend has it, was used by Tenskwatawa as a lookout point during the battle. Beyond you'll roll over the fertile farmland that made this territory so valuable.

Expect to find steep hills in the 100-foot range anytime you get near the rivers. One of the first you'll encounter takes you across the Tippecanoe on Bicycle Bridge Road. The road's unique name came from an old narrow bridge that used to stand over the Wabash; the joke was that only bicycles were thin enough to get across. The road takes you into the town of Delphi, where the Lantern Room Restaurant on the north side of the courthouse square has luncheon specials that are popular with bicyclists.

You'll find scenic views of the Wabash near Georgetown and on the Tow Path Road along the way back. The towpath was part of the old Wabash-Erie Canal, but little evidence of it is left today. Coming into Pittsburg you can enjoy refreshment that once slaked the thirst of the canal boatmen. A flowing, artesian spring still bubbles up with cold, clear water.

The Basics

Start: Park at the Battlefield Interpretive Center on 9th St. Rd., 6 miles north of West Lafayette.
Length: 39.6, 66.6, or 98.8 miles.
Terrain: Flat, rolling, and hilly.

Food: There are restaurants and a grocery in Battle Ground. In Delphi you'll find restaurants, groceries, and a Dairy Queen. There's a soft drink machine at the fire station in Georgetown, and you'll find a restaurant and grocery in Idaville. In the village of Pittsburg, you'll find a flowing spring and two restaurants. In Americus are a restaurant and a pizza shop.

For more information: Wabash River Bicycle Club, c/o Lynn Hodson, 2033 North, 500 East, Lafayette, IN 47905; (317) 743–3506. Greater Lafayette Convention and Visitors Bureau, 301 Frontage Rd., Lafayette, IN 47905; (800) 872–6648.

Bicycle service: In West Lafayette and Lafayette.

Miles & Directions

- 0.0 Ride out of Battlefield Interpretive Center parking lot.
- 0.1 Left on 9th St. Rd.
- 0.3 Left on Prophets Rock Rd. in the village of Battle Ground, where you'll find restaurants and a grocery.
- 1.2 Right on County 600N—short, steep 100 feet.
- 2.0 Straight across Rte. 43 on County 600N.
- 4.5 Right on County 50W, which becomes County 100W.
- 9.3 Right on County 1250S.
- 12.2 Straight across Rte. 43 on County 1250S.
- 15.2 Right on County 300E.
- 15.7 Left on County 1300S. **Caution: Significant traffic may be encountered.**
- 17.2 Left on Springboro Rd.
- 17.7 Right on Bicycle Bridge Rd.
- 23.0 Straight across Rte. 18 onto Franklin St. in Delphi, where you'll find restaurants, groceries, and a Dairy Queen.
- 23.4 Left on Market St. if you are riding the 66.6- or the 98.8-mile route.

If you are riding the 39.6-mile route, continue straight, and turn right at mile 23.5 on Washington St. At mile 23.6 turn right on Water St., and pick up the directions below at mile 82.6.

- 23.8 Right on Adams St., which becomes County 700W (Carrollton Rd.).
- 27.7 Right on County 675N.
- 31.1 Left on County 350W.
- 32.6 Right on County 850N, which becomes County 250W.
- 35.0 Right on County 1050N at French Post Park if you are riding the 98.8-mile route. You'll find water and restrooms at the park.

If you are riding the 66.6-mile route, turn left and cross the Wabash River into Lockport. At mile 35.5 turn left on Tow Path Rd. Continue straight on Tow Path Rd. at mile 38.6, and pick up the directions below at mile 70.6.

- 39.3 Left on County 675W.
- 41.0 Left on Georgetown Rd. across the Wabash River into the village of Georgetown, where you'll find a soft drink machine at the fire station.
- 41.3 Right on an unnamed road.
- 44.9 Straight across U.S. Hwy. 24 onto County 400W.
- 47.4 Left on County 150N, which becomes County 500W.
- 49.5 Right on County 50N.
- 52.3 Right on County 800W.
- 52.8 Left on County 100N.
- 55.8 Left on County 1100W (County Line Rd.).
- 56.9 Right on U.S. Hwy. 24. **Caution: Significant traffic may be encountered.**
- 57.3 Straight on an unnamed road as you enter Burnettsville and U.S. Hwy. 24 veers to the left.
- 57.6 Right on County 1400E.
- 59.4 Left on County 250N.
- 61.9 Left on County 1150E into Idaville, where you'll find a restaurant and a grocery.
- 64.2 Left at Division Rd. onto Springtown Rd.
- 66.2 Right on County 500W.
- 70.6 Right on Tow Path Rd.
- 73.1 Right on County 700W.

- 73.3 Left on County 700N.
- 74.7 Left on County 800W, which becomes County 525N.
- 77.2 Left on County 900W. **Use caution on the steep downhill before town.**
- 79.5 Straight across U.S. 421 onto County 900W in the village of Pittsburg, where you'll find a flowing spring and two restaurants. County 900W becomes County 950W. **Use caution on the steep hill before Bicycle Bridge Rd.**
- 80.6 Left on Bicycle Bridge Rd.
- 81.9 Straight across Rte. 18 into Delphi.
- 82.4 Right on Washington St.
- 82.6 Right on Water St.
- 82.9 Right on Handlton St., which becomes County 800W (Dayton Rd.).
- 87.4 Right on County 200S, which becomes County 700N in Tippecanoe County.
- 89.4 Proceed straight in the village of Colburn.
- 91.7 Right on County 775E.
- 92.1 Right on Rte. 25 in the village of Americus, where you'll find a restaurant and a pizza shop. **Use caution coming into town: There's a steep hill with a stop sign at the bottom, and you may find significant traffic on Rte. 25.**
- 92.2 Left on Grant Rd.
- 93.6 Left on Pretty Prairie Rd.
- 98.3 Proceed straight across Rte. 225 in the village of Battle Ground.
- 98.7 Right into Battlefield Interpretive Center parking lot.
- 98.8 Arrive at Battlefield Interpretive Center.

6

Amishland Ramble

For more than a decade, the Michiana Bicycle Association (MBA) has sponsored the Amishland and Lakes Bike Tour as a "Nostalgic Weekend" ride through rural Indiana in mid-August. The nostalgia is for an unmechanized lifestyle that is part of most Americans' heritage but far away from our present-day realities. This simple, agrarian way of living is preserved by the Amish folk who farm the fertile Indiana soil around the town of Lagrange. The MBA makes a festive time of it, with an ice cream social on the village green in Howe on Saturday and other activities throughout the weekend. Tour loops ranging from 36 to 69 miles are offered on Saturday and from 26 to 65 miles on Sunday.

The commitment of the Amish to their simple way of living is rooted in their strong religious faith. Spun out of the early years of the Protestant Reformation, the Amish formed as a sect by following the teachings of Jacob Amman. He preached a devotion based on a cohesive family, pacifism, and an agrarian way of life. When Amman was martyred in their native Switzerland, the Amish melded into peasant life in Germany. In the early nineteenth century, many joined the flow of German immigrants to the New World. This area of Indiana was among the early Amish settlements.

You'll find the Amish as you ride south and west on this route. Their boxy, black, horse-drawn buggies are a common sight on the roads. Don't be surprised if you see a whole row of them tied to hitching posts behind the County Courthouse in Lagrange. As you ride, be alert for road damage caused by hoofs and the narrow, steel wheel rims of the buggies. On hot summer days the rims can make grooves in the pavement that become permanent hazards for narrow bike tires.

You're likely to see the Amish working the land in their traditional way as you ride along. They still harvest their wheat with muscle power by rhythmically swinging scythes and gathering and tying the grain into shocks to dry in the fields. You'll see them on weekdays, that is. Saturday is for going to town, and Sunday is strictly the Lord's day. They have no telephones, electricity, or motor vehicles. For the most part, if something isn't mentioned in the Bible, they leave it alone. They don't like having their photos taken, as it harks of worldly vanity, but there's no objection to photographing their farms, buggies, or animals.

South of Lagrange you can stop at Yoder's Little Country Store, on Hawpatch Road, for a close look at Amish crafts. You'll be captivated by the beautiful designs of the quilts the local Amish women hand-stitch. A visit to Yoder's will give you a feel for the industry and skill that mark the lifestyle of the Amish. Don't bother calling ahead—there's no phone. On County 550S you'll pass David Rogers Park, site of several restored pioneer log cabins and a favorite picnic spot of the Amish. Not a bad place for you to take a break either.

The Basics

Start: Park on Union St. at 4th St., 2 miles south of I–80/90 in the town of Howe.
Length: 31.0 miles.
Terrain: Flat to gently rolling.
Food: There are restaurants and an ice cream shop in Howe. In Lagrange there are several restaurants, a bakery, and a Dairy Queen.
For more information: Amishland and Lakes Bike Tour, Michiana Bicycle Assn., 56085 Cedar Rd., Mishawaka, IN 46545; (219) 256–6735. La Grange County Chamber of Commerce, 512 N. Detroit St., Lagrange, IN 46761; (219) 463–2443.

Miles & Directions

- 0.0 Ride north on 4th St. from the intersection of Union St.

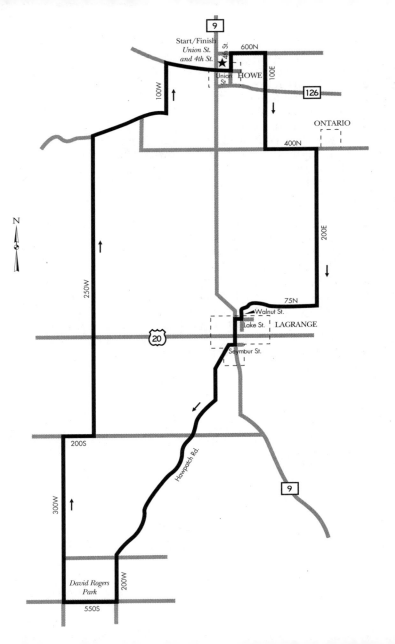

- 0.4 Right on County 600N.
- 1.0 Right on County 100E.
- 3.1 Left on County 400N.
- 4.1 Right on County 200E.
- 7.4 Right on County 75N.
- 8.8 Left on Walnut St. at intersection with Nursery Rd.
- 9.1 Right on Lake St. in the town of Lagrange, where you'll find several restaurants, a bakery, and a Dairy Queen.
- 9.3 Left on Rte. 9 (Detroit St.).
- 9.7 Right on Seymour St.
- 9.8 Left on Hawpatch Rd.
- 14.9 Straight on County 200W.
- 15.9 Right on County 550S.
- 16.9 Right on County 300W.
- 20.4 Right on County 200S.
- 20.9 Left on County 250W.
- 27.1 Right at the T intersection on an unnamed road that becomes County 100W as it turns north.
- 29.7 Right on an unnamed road that becomes Union St. in Howe.
- 31.0 Arrive at Union St. and 4th St.

7

Hoosier Hills Challenge

Bloomington is the home of Indiana University and, for over twenty years, an outstanding ride named the Hoosier Hills Bike Tour. Held annually on the first weekend of June, the ride attracts people from around the Midwest to enjoy the scenery and challenge of the southern Indiana hill country.

Bloomington is also where the classic 1979 coming-of-age movie *Breaking Away* was filmed. "Breaking away" is a bicycle-racing phrase that means to separate yourself from the pack. In the movie the lead character, Dave Stoller, played by Dennis Christopher, learns lessons about life from the seat of a bicycle. He's a town boy, a "cutter," as the locals are called, for the once prominent trade of stone cutting at the many area limestone quarries. Dave tries to fit into the university and bike-racing scene by affecting an Italian accent, before some hard knocks make him realize how important his real friends and family are. *Breaking Away* was filmed exclusively in the Bloomington area and features a number of scenes of bicycling in the city and countryside.

You can try your own breakaway as you test your legs in the hilly terrain south of Bloomington. The ride will be easy on you in the beginning. You'll roll along Knight Ridge and Rush Ridge before entering the woods of the Hoosier National Forest, where wild turkey, deer, and bald eagles are sometimes seen. Soon you'll drop 250 feet to the 0.5-mile-long Salt Creek Causeway crossing Monroe Lake. The causeway divides Indiana's largest lake into a no-wake area to the east, where fishing is popular, and the western area, where power boating and waterskiing are common. You can expect an even steeper grade climbing up from the lake to Dutch Ridge. If the terrain is too much for you, the 42-mile option on Chapel Hill Road will cut the remaining steep climbs to one.

If you continue south, you'll be in for more forest scenery and a long downhill run into the valley of Little Salt Creek before a 200-foot climb to Heltonville. If you didn't already know Indiana is crazy about basketball, you'll figure it out when you see a sign on the outskirts of the tiny village proclaiming Heltonville the home of Damon Bailey. Bailey was a guard on the Indiana basketball team whom coach Bobby Knight spotted as a future prospect when he saw him play as an eighth-grader in Heltonville. Now, that's pride! There's a country store that serves sandwiches in Heltonville, and if you like to talk about basketball, you should get along fine with the locals.

West of Heltonville the route rolls along the valley of Leatherwood Creek before turning north and crossing moderate hills over to the Salt Creek Valley. You can take a break or go for a swim at the Salt Creek–Monroe Dam before the last 200-foot climb east of Smithville. Once on top it's an easy roll back to Bloomington, unless, of course, you're breaking away.

The Basics

Start: Park at Winslow Park, on Winslow Rd. on the south side of Bloomington.

Length: 42.0 or 57.7 miles.

Terrain: Rolling to hilly.

Food: There are numerous food options in Bloomington but few on the route. At the intersection of Rte. 446 and Chapel Hill Rd., you'll find a country store. In Heltonville there is a country store that serves sandwiches. The city of Bedford is only 1 mile off the route from the intersection of Rte. 58 and Mt. Pleasant Rd. if the need for food or other services arises. At the dam on Monroe Lake, you'll find bait-and-tackle shops with soft drink machines. There is a country store in Smithville.

For more information: Hoosier Hills Tour, c/o Bloomington Bicycle Club, P.O. Box 463, Bloomington, IN 47402; (812) 331–0001. Bloomington/Monroe County Convention & Visitors Bureau, 2855 N. Walnut St., Bloomington, IN 47404; (800) 800–0037.

Bicycle service: Numerous shops in Bloomington.

Miles & Directions

- 0.0 Ride south out of the Winslow Park parking lot.
- 0.3 Left on Winslow Rd., which becomes High St.
- 0.8 Right on Rogers Rd. at the intersection with High St.; Rogers Rd. becomes Smith Rd.
- 3.2 Right on Moores Pike Rd.
- 3.7 Right on Rte. 446 (Knight Ridge Rd.). **Caution: Significant traffic may be encountered.**
- 14.4 Straight on Rte. 446 at the intersection with Chapel Hill Rd., where you'll find a country store.

If you are riding the 42.0-mile route, turn right on Chapel Hill Rd., which becomes Guthrie Rd. At mile 17.6 turn right on Guthrie Rd. in the village of Chapel Hill. At mile 24.5 turn right on Hansom Rd. From here pick up the directions below at mile 40.2.

- 21.9 Right on Rte. 58.
- 22.5 Left on Rte. 58 in Heltonville, where you'll find a country store that serves sandwiches.
- 30.2 Right on Mt. Pleasant Rd.
- 36.6 Straight in the village of Logan.
- 37.2 Right on an unnamed road.
- 39.6 Right on Hansom Rd. in the village of Guthrie.
- 40.2 Straight on Hansom Rd. at the intersection with Guthrie Rd. Hansom Rd. becomes Valley Mission Rd.
- 42.9 Straight on Dam Site Rd. at the dam on Monroe Lake, where you'll find bait-and-tackle shops with soft drink machines.
- 43.8 Right on Strain Ridge Rd at the intersection with Hobart Rd.
- 44.3 Right on Strain Ridge Rd. at the intersection with Monroe Lake Rd.
- 48.2 Right on Smithville Rd. in the village of Smithville, where you'll find a country store.
- 48.4 Straight on Ramp Creek Rd.
- 50.7 Left on Handy Rd.
- 52.2 Bear right on Harrel Rd. in the village of Handy.

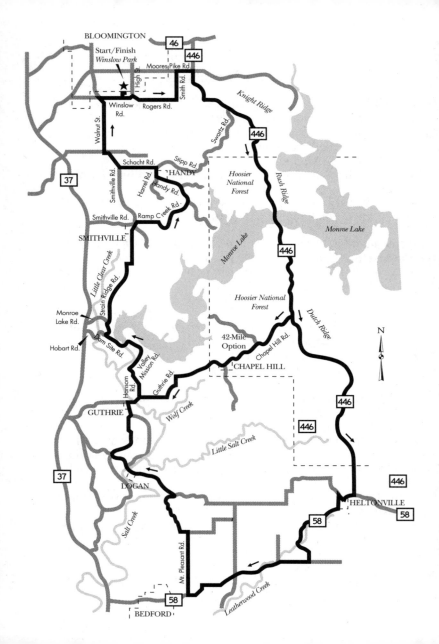

- 52.5 Left on Schacht Rd.
- 53.8 Right on Smithville Rd.
- 54.6 Right on Walnut Pike, which becomes Walnut St. in Bloomington.
- 56.7 Right on Winslow Rd.
- 57.4 Left into Winslow Park.
- 57.7 Arrive at parking lot.

8

Great Pumpkin Ramble

In the nineteenth century German immigrants had a great influence on young America. Their industry, skillfulness, and, often, Catholic religion combined with a fun-loving appreciation of song, food, and drink to take the harsh edge off frontier life. Much of German culture in this country was repressed during World War I, and it's often hard to identify it in the nation's mix today.

In the rural Midwest, though, there are pockets of German settlements that retain some of the character the settlers brought from the old country. The small villages around Evansville are just such places. The land the Germans chose is the setting for the Great Pumpkin Metric, which for the past twelve years has offered this 50-kilometer tour, as well as 100- and 25-kilometer routes, on the first Sunday of October.

Tall Gothic church spires that can be seen for miles away are the marks of rural German villages. St. Joseph, St. Wendell, and Darmstadt serve much the same purpose as villages in the old country. They are centers of religion and social life. The social life centers around the village's other prominent structure, the tavern. In Europe the villages would have contained clusters of houses and barns; farmers would have lived in town and gone out to work the land, a holdover from the medieval system when the workers didn't own the land. In America they were free to build on their own land, but the village remained the heart of their community.

As you ride on smoothly paved roads past the neat, productive farms planted with corn, winter wheat, and beans, you'll appreciate the attention to detail that characterizes the Germans. Encounters with the locals on the roads are usually pleasant, but if you really want to meet them on their own turf, you've got to stop at a tavern. These are gathering places that serve food as well as beer.

Don't be surprised to see children running around, because in the German tradition taverns are family places.

The Silver Bell in St. Wendell and the Darmstadt Inn in Darmstadt are good choices. The typical German fare isn't for those worried about cholesterol. You might want to pass on the brain sandwich, but you'll regret it if you don't try catfish fiddlers. Five dollars will get you a hefty serving of these small, deep-fried catfish, with a side of German fried potatoes and a stein of Gerst beer, a German-style lager brewed only in Evansville. Gerst sponsors a bicycle racing team, too.

You'll have to deal with a few hills in the 100-foot range in the heavily wooded areas east and west of St. Joseph, but if you wait until St. Wendell to take a break, you'll have only moderate rolling terrain left to ride on the way back to the 4-H Center.

The Basics

Start: Park at the Vanderburgh County 4-H Center, 0.25 mile west of U.S. Hwy. 41.
Length: 31.8 miles.
Terrain: Flat to rolling.
Food: This is the tavern tour. You'll find food at taverns in St. Joseph, St. Wendell, and Darmstadt.
For more information: Great Pumpkin Metric, Evansville Bicycle Club, 20 E. Florida St., Evansville, IN 47711; (812) 426–1330. Evansville Convention & Visitors Bureau, 401 S.E. Riverside Dr., Evansville, IN 47708; (800) 433–3025.
Bicycle service: In nearby Evansville.

Miles & Directions

- 0.0 Ride north from the Vanderburgh County 4-H Center.
- 0.2 Left on Boonville–New Harmony Rd.
- 0.3 Right on Martin Rd.
- 1.2 Left on Inglefield Rd.

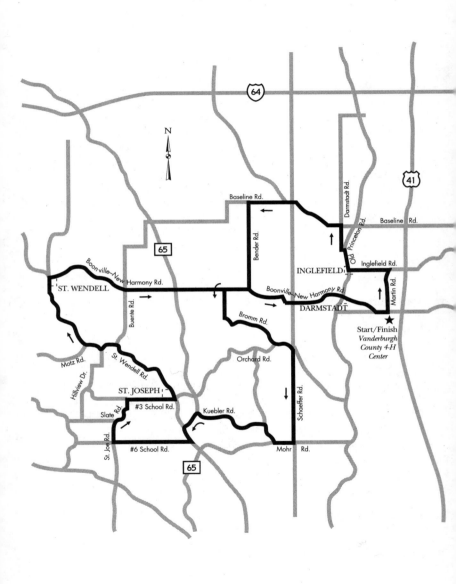

- 2.1 Right on Old Princeton Rd. in the village of Inglefield.
- 2.4 Left on Darmstadt Rd.
- 3.1 Left on Baseline Rd.
- 5.3 Left on Bender Rd.
- 7.2 Right on Boonville–New Harmony Rd.
- 7.9 Left on Bromm Rd.
- 9.8 Left on Orchard Rd.
- 10.0 Right on Schaeffer Rd.
- 12.2 Right on Mohr Rd.
- 12.4 Right on Kuebler Rd.
- 12.8 Bear left on Kuebler Rd.
- 14.5 Left on Rte. 65. **Caution: Ride on the paved shoulder; significant traffic may be encountered.**
- 15.2 Right on #6 School Rd.
- 16.9 Right on St. Joe Rd.
- 17.4 Right on Slate Rd.
- 18.2 Right on #3 School Rd.
- 19.2 Left on St. Wendell Rd. in the village of St. Joseph, where you'll find a tavern.
- 23.7 Right on Boonville–New Harmony Rd. in the village of St. Wendell, where you'll find a tavern.
- 26.7 Straight across U.S. Hwy. 65 on Boonville–New Harmony Rd.
- 27.0 Use caution crossing rough railroad tracks.
- 30.4 Straight on Boonville–New Harmony Rd. in the village of Darmstadt, where you'll find a tavern.
- 31.6 Right to Vanderburgh County 4-H Center.
- 31.8 Arrive at Vanderburgh County 4-H Center.

Iowa

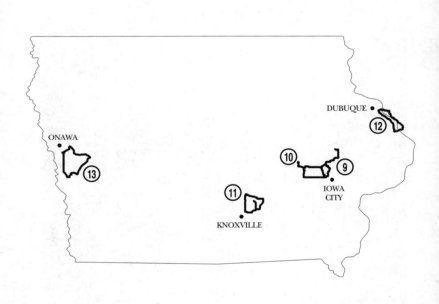

Iowa

9

Lincoln Highway Challenge

If you, like Tom Conway, are into exploring historic roadways, you might do as he has and organize a ride for your local bike club. So what if there are a few hills along the way, including the infamous Sugarbottom Hill? For Conway, who has climbed the massive Galibier on the Tour de France route, old Sugarbottom is just a prairie pimple. The Lincoln Highway Challenge isn't an annually scheduled event; rather, it's just another excuse for the Bicyclists of Iowa City club to get together and ride through the scenic countryside.

The goal, of course, is to ride on the Lincoln Highway, but to get there some miles must be covered first. The ride starts in Iowa City, the location of the University of Iowa and the original state capital. Heading north out of town, you'll hit a succession of 75- to 120-foot wooded hills. Even the dread Sugarbottom is only about 100 feet, but it comes in 0.2 mile.

Once up on the ridge, you'll pass the road to the MacBride Raptor Center, a nice side trip of about 0.75 mile, if you're interested in birds of prey. The center rescues raptors that have been hit by cars, shot, or injured in some other way and does what can be done to heal them and return them to the wild. Birds that can't be released are kept at the center and can be viewed.

After an easy roll through typical Iowa farmland, you'll come to Solon, where you'll find Jonesie's Cafe, famed for its tenderloin sandwiches. If you're there early on a Saturday when there's a home football game at the university, you might catch the brunch at the Methodist Church just off Main St. Church members put out the spread for the football fans, but hungry bicyclists are welcome, too. In Sutliffe you can take a break at the old stressed-iron bridge over the Cedar River. When the new bridge was built, the old one was turned into a picnic area.

At Lisbon you finally reach the old Lincoln Highway, the first transcontinental highway in the world. It was called Main Street USA because it went through so many small towns on its way from New York to San Francisco. In fact, the old stretch of highway is Main Street between Lisbon and Mt. Vernon.

At the dawn of the automobile era, most rural roads were poorly marked and impassable for part of the year. In 1912 auto manufacturer Carl J. Fisher promoted the idea of a transcontinental highway. Work began in 1914, and a year later none other than Emily Post, etiquette adviser to propriety-conscious America, boarded a touring car in New York heading for the Panama Pacific Exhibition in San Francisco.

The highway was dedicated as a memorial to Abraham Lincoln, and in 1926 it became U.S. Highway 30. On September 1, 1928, troops of Boy Scouts erected more than 3,000 concrete mile markers all across the country. The markers bore a brass medallion of Lincoln. One of the few remaining can be seen under the water tower in the little park at the ride turnaround point.

The short section of the Lincoln Highway you'll ride is lined with old trees and houses. There's hardly any traffic on it. Anyone traveling transcontinental and not overhead in an airliner is doing 65 down on I–80. The old road is a reminder of the days when setting out in a car was an adventure. It was a time when you might come back from a trip with the memory of a first-rate hot roast beef sandwich at a cafe like Gwen's in Lisbon. Today it seems hard to remember which interstate exit McDonald's you ate at last.

The Basics

Start: Park on the street and begin riding from College Green Park, at the intersection of College St. and Dodge St. in downtown Iowa City.
Length: 65.6 miles.
Terrain: Rolling to hilly.
Food: There are many food options in Iowa City. In Solon you'll find a convenience store and a cafe. There is a tavern in Sutliffe. In Lisbon you'll find a cafe. There are restaurants and a grocery in Mt.

Vernon. North Liberty has a grocery store and an ice cream shop. In Coralville you'll find restaurants and a grocery store.

For more information: Bicyclists of Iowa City, Inc., P.O. Box 846, Iowa City, IA 52244; (319) 338–1575. Iowa City Chamber of Commerce, 325 E. Washington, P.O. Box 2358, Iowa City, IA 52244; (319) 337–9637.

Bicycle service: In Iowa City.

Miles & Directions

- 0.0 Ride east on College St. from the intersection of College St. and Dodge St. at College Green Park.
- 0.2 Left on Governor St. N.
- 0.9 Right on Dewey St.
- 1.1 Right on Summit St. N.
- 1.4 Straight across Rte. 1 onto Prairie du Chien Rd.
- 3.9 Bear right on N.E. Newport Rd. at the Y intersection. The road to the left dead-ends at the Coralville Reservoir.
- 6.7 Left on N.E. Sugarbottom Rd. (if you pass a little white church, you've gone the wrong way).
- 9.1 Left on N.E. Sugarbottom Rd.
- 12.2 Right on County F–28.
- 12.4 Proceed straight at the road to the MacBride Raptor Center.
- 16.4 Left on Rte. 1 in the town of Solon, where you'll find a convenience store and a cafe.
- 17.1 Right on County F–14, the only paved road to the right in Solon.
- 23.8 Left on County X–20 in the village of Sutliffe, where you'll find a tavern.
- 29.3 Straight across U.S. Hwy. 30 onto County X–20.
- 29.5 Left on Main St. in the town of Lisbon, where you'll find a cafe.
- 31.2 Straight across Rte. 1 onto Main St. in the town of Mt. Vernon, where you'll find restaurants and a grocery.
- 31.7 Straight at the traffic light onto Main St. where County X–20 turns right.

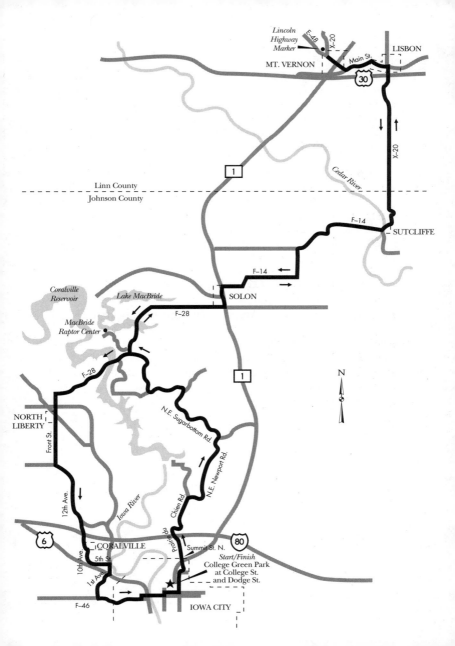

- 31.8 Turn around at the small park with a water tower across from Cornell College.
- 34.1 Right on County X–20 in Lisbon.
- 34.3 Straight across U.S. Hwy. 30 onto County X–20.
- 40.1 Right on County F–14 in Sutliffe.
- 46.7 Left on Rte. 1 in Solon.
- 47.4 Right on County F–28.
- 51.6 Right on County F–28.
- 55.3 Straight across N. Dubuque St. onto Front St. in the village of North Liberty, where you'll find a grocery store and an ice cream shop. Front St. becomes 12th Ave. in Coralville.
- 60.3 Right on 10th Ave.
- 60.7 Left on 5th St. in the town of Coralville, where you'll find restaurants and a grocery store.
- 61.4 Right on 1st Ave.
- 62.8 Left on County F–46 (Melrose Ave.).
- 64.3 Left on Grand Ave. S.
- 64.4 Right on Grand Ave., which becomes Burlington St. after crossing the Iowa River.
- 65.1 Left on Linn St.
- 65.2 Right on College St.
- 65.6 Arrive at College Green Park at College St. and Dodge St.

10

Amana Cruise

The rolling corn country of Iowa is home to a unique collection of small villages known as the Amana Colony. Each year the Bicyclists of Iowa City organize a tour to the colony on the Fourth of July. It's a good destination for cyclists: People know how to eat in Amana.

The name Amana has been synonymous with craftsmanship for more than a hundred years. In 1855 members of the communal German Protestant sect known as the Church of True Inspiration began farming the land along the Iowa River. They chose to name the colony Amana, which means to remain true, from the Song of Solomon. Self-sufficiency was the goal of each of seven villages that made up the colony. The simple industries that made them so produced surpluses that could be sold to add to the colony's success. The colonists' furniture, woolens, meats, and sausages gained a reputation for quality among thrifty, no-nonsense Iowans.

While communal living ceased in 1932, German continued to be the primary language. New York Yankees pitcher Bill Zuber, an Amana boy who retired in 1948 to operate a restaurant in Homestead after ten seasons in the majors, had to learn English when he left the colony.

The townsfolk still hold to their roots in Amana, and people flock there to buy products from appliances to beer, all made with craftsmanship that seems forgotten in much of America. Nowhere is the importance of tradition more apparent than at the many restaurants in the colony. The Ox Yoke and the Colony Inn are two favorites of bicyclists at the route turnaround in Amana. Expect to find typical German country fare such as sauerbraten and Wiener schnitzel served home-style, with big bowls of sauerkraut and potatoes.

The route to and from Amana covers typical rolling Iowa farm-land that inspired the artist Grant Wood. Riding east in Iowa City, you'll cross the Iowa River and climb up Grand Avenue through the beautiful University of Iowa campus before heading out on County F–46. Then you're in corn country. The road runs straight as an arrow, and you'll zip down one 60- to 90-foot hill and up the next. The crops you'll see aren't so linear. The plowing and planting follow the contours of the hills to help control erosion, and the sinuous bands are an agricultural art form.

The Basics

Start: Park on the street and begin riding from College Green Park, at the intersection of College St. and Dodge St. in downtown Iowa City.
Length: 59.0 miles.
Terrain: Gently rolling.
Food: There are numerous food opportunities in Iowa City. At Oxford you'll find a convenience store. There are restaurants and a convenience store in Homestead. In Amana there are restaurants, a convenience store, and an ice cream shop. In North Liberty you'll find a grocery store and an ice cream shop. There are restaurants and a grocery store in Coralville.
For more information: Bicyclists of Iowa City, P.O. Box 846, Iowa City, IA 52244. Iowa City Chamber of Commerce, 325 E. Washington, P.O. Box 2358, Iowa City, IA 52244; (319) 337–9637.
Bicycle service: Several shops in Iowa City.

Miles & Directions

- 0.0 Ride west on College St. at the intersection of College St. and Dodge St. at College Green Park.
- 0.4 Left on Linn St.
- 0.5 Right on Burlington St., which becomes Grand Ave. when it crosses the Iowa River.

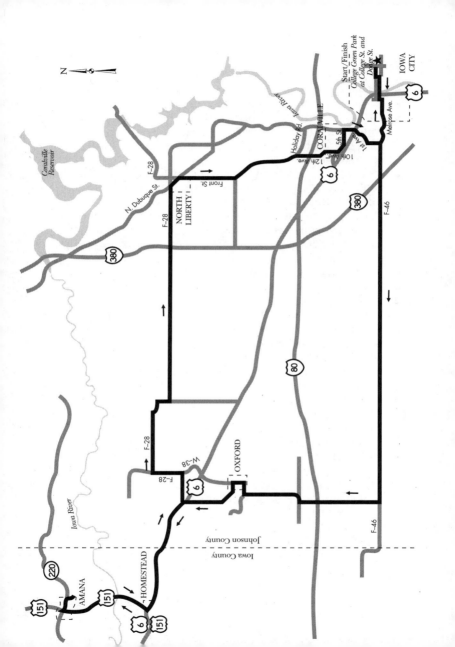

- 1.2 Left on Grand Ave. S.
- 1.4 Right on Melrose Ave., which becomes County F–46.
- 14.9 Right at the sign directing you to the town of Oxford.
- 20.0 Left at the telephone company in the village of Oxford, where you'll find a convenience store.
- 21.8 Left on U.S. Hwy. 6. **Caution: Significant traffic may be encountered.**
- 25.7 Right on U.S. Hwy. 151 in the village of Homestead, where you'll find restaurants and a convenience store. **Caution: Significant traffic may be encountered.**
- 28.7 Right on Rte. 220 in the village of Amana, where you'll find restaurants, a convenience store, and an ice cream shop.
- 29.0 Bear right on an unnamed street that is known to the locals as Main St. Amana.
- 29.3 Turn around at the Colony Inn restaurant.
- 29.6 Left on Rte. 220.
- 29.9 Left on U.S. Hwy. 151.
- 32.9 Left on U.S. Hwy. 6.
- 36.7 Left on an unnamed road just past two large blue silos on the opposite side of the highway.
- 37.8 Left on County F–28.
- 48.4 Right on N. Dubuque St. in the town of North Liberty, where you'll find a grocery store and an ice cream shop.
- 48.8 Right on Front St., which becomes 12th Ave. in Coralville.
- 53.7 Right on 10th Ave.
- 54.1 Left on 5th St. in the town of Coralville, where you'll find restaurants and a grocery store.
- 54.8 Right on 1st Ave.
- 56.2 Left on Melrose Ave.
- 57.8 Left on Grand Ave. S.
- 57.9 Right on Grand Ave., which becomes Burlington St. when you cross the Iowa River.
- 58.5 Left on Linn St.
- 58.6 Right on College St.
- 59.0 Arrive at College Green Park.

11

Another Dam Bike Ramble

Knoxville's claim to fame is that it's the sprint car capital of the world. So what are sprint cars, and what've they got to do with bicycling? Well, they're tiny race cars with big engines and air foils, and they usually blast around dirt track ovals like the Knoxville Raceway, except on the first Saturday of October. That's the annual date for Another Dam Bike Tour, and the throng of cyclists is led out of town by one of these highly tuned, internal combustion thoroughbreds.

The rest of the tour is a much quieter experience. The route takes you around a feature not usually associated with Iowa: a big lake. Thanks to the Army Corps of Engineers' dam, Lake Red Rock is the largest lake in Iowa. In fact, during the Flood of 1993 it was the third largest body of water outside of the Great Lakes. The dam is also responsible for this tour's unique name.

The dam held back the water of the Des Moines River, though it's on the wrong side of the city of the same name to save it. The lake came within 4 inches of capacity, and you could feel the dam shake as 110,000 cubic feet of water per second passed over its spillways. An unusual effect of the flood was the presence of large flocks of pelicans that are typically seen only during the fall migration.

Riding north from Knoxville you'll pass the Sprint Car Hall of Fame and the raceway before descending Hollingshead Hill into the Whitebreast Creek bottom, where you'll have a chance to see herons in flight against the background of red rock bluffs. Soon you'll be rolling over the only mile-long bridge in Iowa. To the west you can see Principal Tower in Des Moines, 40 miles away.

From the bridge you can also see the Painted Rock Bluffs, on the north shore of Lake Red Rock. The bluffs were once the wintering grounds of the Fox Indians and are now part of Elk Rock State Park. The route also passes three federal and two county parks. G–28 is part of the Dragoon Trail, the route explored by Colonel Stephen Kearny in 1835. It was once an overland stage route and is lined with historical farms.

Crossing the Red Rock Dam, you can contrast the lake scenery on the right with the broad, natural river valley on the left. At the south end of the dam is an overlook, as well as a visitor center with displays of area history and wildlife. The 4-mile out-and-back excursion to Whitebreast Recreation Area is worth it for the overview of the lake. From this point you can see nearly all of the lakeshore. On T–15 you'll pass woods, farms, and pastures. The last 6 miles are on Old Pella Road, a narrow, tree-lined lane.

The Basics

Start: Park at Auld Park at 2nd St. and Reno St., 3 blocks north of Business 92 in Knoxville.
Length: 36.8 miles.
Terrain: Rolling.
Food: There are several groceries and restaurants, including the ubiquitous Dairy Queen, in Knoxville.
For more information: Another Dam Bike Ride, c/o Knoxville Chamber of Commerce, P.O. Box 337, Knoxville, IA 50138; (515) 828–7555.

Miles & Directions

- 0.0 Ride north on 2nd St. from the Auld Park parking lot at the corner of 2nd St. and Reno St.
- 0.1 Left on Rock Island St.
- 0.8 Right on Hwy. 14 (Lincoln St.). **Caution: Significant traffic may be encountered early morning and late afternoon.**
- 8.8 Right on G–28.
- 16.8 Right on T–15.

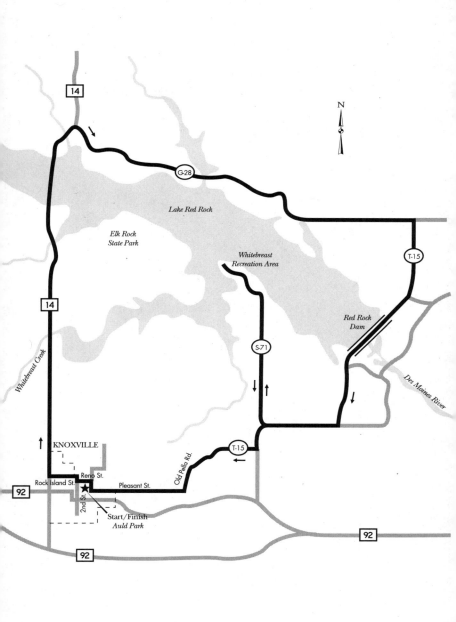

- 23.4 Right on S–71.
- 27.4 Turn around at Whitebreast Recreation Area overlook.
- 31.5 Right on T–15, which becomes Old Pella Rd. and then Pleasant St. in Knoxville.
- 36.4 Left on Reno St.
- 36.8 Arrive at Auld Park.

12

Tour of the Mississippi River Valley Classic

The Tour of the Mississippi River Valley (TOMRV) is your opportunity to enjoy terrific scenery and take on the challenge of the tough terrain created by the great river and its tributaries. It's also a step back in time because many of the sleepy little towns retain much of the character from the early days of settlement, when the Mississippi was the route to the frontier.

This route combines the northern sections of the two-day TOMRV event into a one-day loop. TOMRV is organized by the Quad Cities Bicycle Club in Davenport and is always held the second weekend of June. The tour, which attracts more than 1,000 riders, runs from Bettendorf (one of the Quad Cities) to Dubuque for the overnight and returns the following day.

As presented here the route begins in Dubuque, a river town with roots deep enough to reach back to the days when Spain possessed the territory. Heading south you'll tackle a 200- and a 400-foot climb before reaching the river flats at the picturesque town of Bellevue. A 250- and a 50-foot climb are necessary to take you inland over the Iowa farm country to the quiet town of Preston. From there it's a rolling cross-country trek back to the Mississippi and the island community of Sabula.

Crossing the Illinois shore you'll have a few miles of flat as you skirt the edge of towering bluffs called the Mississippi Palisades and follow the Apple River Valley to the town of Hanover. Grabbing some energy food in Hanover is a good idea. Just outside of town you begin a long, gradual 350-foot climb up Blackjack Road. Be careful on the steep descent. You'll lose all of that elevation in less than a mile.

One of the tour's highlights is a visit to Galena. If it weren't for the cars and your modern bicycle, you'd think you'd found a Civil War–era town frozen in amber. Galena bloomed in the 1840s when 80 percent of the nation's lead-mining production was loaded onto its steamboats. The town's decline began when skilled miners got word of the California gold rush. The playing out of lead deposits and a newfangled thing called a railroad hastened the bust. The Civil War didn't help either, though the town provided nine generals for the Union Army.

The most famous of these was Ulysses S. Grant, although he was hardly known when the war started. By that time Grant's military career was washed up and he was working in his father's harness shop to make ends meet. When he marched off, the only ones who missed him were his family and the corner saloon keeper. When he came home, he was the savior of the Union and the grateful town gave him the fine, red brick Victorian home he lived in until he was elected president in 1868. The home is now a State Historic Site open for tours.

Just think of this tour as out-of-town, out-of-the-saddle. Leaving Galena you'll face three 200-foot climbs and descents before the long, fast run into Dubuque. The workout isn't over until you've climbed back out of the valley to Clarke College. You'll see why Dubuque is one of the few midwestern towns with a cable car.

The Basics

Start: Park on Clarke Drive at Clarke College, 0.5 mile west of U.S. Hwy. 52 (Central Avenue) in Dubuque.
Length: 108.3 miles.
Terrain: Rolling to very hilly.
Food: There are many food choices in Dubuque. In St. Donatus you'll find a restaurant. Bellevue has a restaurant and an ice cream shop. There are restaurants and convenience stores in Preston and Sabula. Just off-route in Savanna you'll find restaurants and fast-food shops. Hanover also has several restaurants and fast-food shops. There are many restaurants and several ice cream shops in Galena.

For more information: Quad Cities Bicycle Club, c/o Suzie LaForce, 2023 E. 45th St., Davenport, IA 52807; (319) 355–5530. Dubuque Convention and Visitors Bureau, 770 Town Clock Plaza, Dubuque, IA 52001; (800) 79–VISIT.

Miles & Directions

- 0.0 Head southwest on Clarke Dr. from Clarke College.
- 0.4 Left on Grandview Ave.
- 3.0 Right on Rockdale Rd. immediately before the intersection of Grandview and U.S. Hwy. 61/151/52. **Caution: Downhill sections on Rockdale Rd. have potholes and rough surfaces.**
- 4.7 Left on the short connector road to U.S. Hwy. 52 near the top of the hill. If you go past Happy's, you've missed it.
- 5.0 Straight onto U.S. Hwy. 52 at the traffic light at U.S. Hwy. 61/151.
- 15.3 Proceed straight in the village of St. Donatus, where you'll find a restaurant.
- 25.1 Proceed straight in the town of Bellevue, where you'll find a restaurant, grocery, and ice cream shop, as well as a water pump in a city park along the riverfront.
- 30.6 Turn right on County Z–34.
- 41.9 Turn left on Rte. 64 in the town of Preston, where you'll find a restaurant and a convenience store off-route.
- 46.1 Continue straight on Rte. 64 through the crossroads village of Miles, where you'll find a soft drink machine.
- 54.5 Left onto Rte. 64 at the three-way intersection in the town of Sabula, where you'll find a restaurant and a convenience store.
- 56.7 **Use caution as you approach the Mississippi River Bridge: The bridge is narrow and steep; you may wish to walk across the steel grate section.**
- 57.5 Turn left onto Rte. 84 at the end of the bridge. The town of Savanna is off-route 0.25 mile to the right; there you'll find several restaurants and fast-food shops.
- 69.2 Follow Rte. 84 through the town of Hanover, where you'll find several restaurants and fast-food shops.

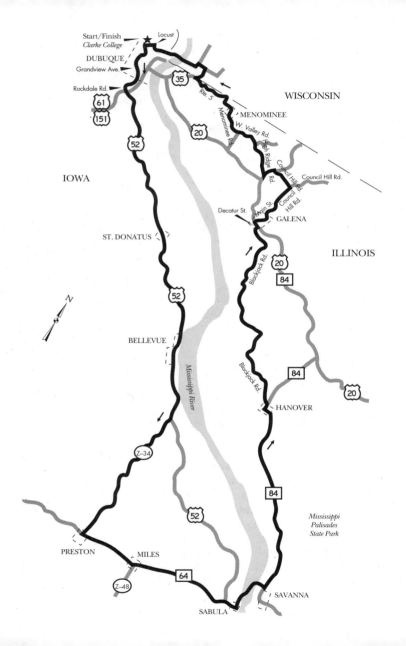

- 71.4 Left onto Blackjack Rd. **Use caution on the steep descent at mile 78.9.**
- 86.6 Left onto U.S. Hwy. 20 (Decatur St.) in the town of Galena.
- 86.9 Right on Main St., where you'll find many restaurants. Main St. becomes Broadway and then Dewey Ave.
- 88.5 Left on Council Hill Rd.
- 90.7 Left on Council Hill Rd. at a T intersection where all three roads have the same name.
- 92.2 Left on Rte. 84. **Caution: Significant traffic may be encountered.**
- 93.0 Right on High Ridge Rd.
- 94.2 Bear left on W. Valley Rd.
- 96.0 Right on Menominee Rd.
- 97.0 Continue straight in the village of Menominee.
- 98.3 Left on Rte. 5.
- 99.7 Follow Rte. 5 to the left.
- 102.2 Right on Hwy. 35; cross the Wisconsin state line.
- 103.0 Left onto U.S. Hwy. 61/151 at four-way stop. **Use caution, and ride on the paved shoulder. Expect heavy traffic and a long steep downhill.**
- 104.7 **Use caution crossing the Mississippi River Bridge. Ride on the wide shoulder and stay away from the grates on the extreme right-hand side of the emergency lane.**
- 105.3 Exit right to Kerper Blvd.
- 106.1 Continue straight as U.S. Hwy. 151 becomes 16th St.
- 106.4 Right on Elm St.; then make an immediate left on 17th St.
- 106.5 Bear right onto Locust St.
- 108.1 Right on Clarke Dr.
- 108.3 Arrive at Clarke College.

13

Onabike Cruise

On the last Saturday of August the small Missouri River Valley town of Onawa hosts the annual Onabike, the largest one-day ride in western Iowa. The 300-plus riders are treated to fine hospitality and scenery as they follow the 62-mile route described here or a 25-mile alternate. On-route they ride over a relic of the last ice age.

When Thomas Jefferson doubled the size of the United States with the Louisiana Purchase, he sent Meriwether Lewis and William Clark off to explore this new possession that stretched from the Mississippi to the Pacific Ocean. Jefferson was not only president but also one of the foremost scientists of the day, and so little was known about the West then that he instructed the explorers to keep an eye out for mastodons. Bones belonging to this long-tusked, elephant-like beast of the glacial era had been excavated in the East. He theorized that the mastodons might not be extinct and perhaps had just moved west.

In August 1804, when Lewis and Clark camped at the site of the park that bears their name a few miles west of Onawa, they were more concerned with finding deserters than mastodons. They'd gotten there via the Missouri on the keelboat *Discovery*, a massive 55-foot-long craft they hoped to sail along with a favorable wind. Often, though it went forward only when pushed by long poles from the deck or towed with ropes from the shore; hence the desertions. A full-sized replica of the keelboat can be viewed in the park.

Pedaling east from Onawa you can see the glacial relic in the distance as Lewis and Clark did from their camp. It's no mastadon, though. You'll be looking at the rolling ridges of the Loess Hills. Their lovely mix of woods and hay fields give the ride its scenic character. The continental glacier was very good at some things, like grinding down mountains and generating weather patterns that certainly would discourage bicycling tourism these days. As it happened, the grinding produced a fine dust called loess (pro-nounced *luss*) and the winds carried it to Iowa by the ton.

The 14,000-year-old Loess Hills are more pretty than formidable. They've eroded considerably, filling the lowland with some of the most fertile soil in the world. You'll skirt the hills at first along Larpenteur Road and then cross them on a gradual 240-foot climb. An easy roll south along the valley of the Soldier River will rest you for the second crossing, steeper than the first but the same height, followed by a screaming descent back into the Missouri Valley flatland. From there, with luck, you can cruise through endless fields of corn and soybeans to Onawa with the wind at your back. After all, its no fun poling or towing a bike.

The Basics

Start: Park in the Gaukel Park parking lot, off of 12th St., 6 blocks north of Hwy. 175 (Iowa St.) in Onawa.

Length: 62.4 miles.

Terrain: Mostly flat with some moderate hills.

Food: There are numerous cafes, groceries, and convenience stores in Onawa. In Soldier, Moorhead, Pisgah, and Little Sioux there are cafes, groceries, and convenience stores. There are a restaurant and a convenience store at Blencoe.

For more information: Onawa Chamber of Commerce, 1009 Iowa Ave., Onawa, IA 51040; (712) 423–1801.

Miles & Directions

- ■ 0.0 Left out of Gaukel Park on 12th St.
- ■ 0.6 Left on Hwy. 175 (Iowa St.).
- ■ 1.7 Left on County L–12.
- ■ 7.4 Right on Larpenteur Rd.
- ■ 12.8 Left on Hwy. 37 in the village of Turin.
- ■ 23.4 Right on Hwy. 183 in the village of Soldier, where you'll find a cafe, grocery, and convenience store.

Start/Finish
Clarke College ONAWA
Lewis and Clark
State Park
12th St.

L–12

175

Larpenter Rd.

175

TURIN

37

SOLDIER

K–45

29

Missouri River

BLENCOE

IOWA

Little Sioux River

MOREHEAD

183

Soldier River

Monona County
Harrison County

F–20

PISGAH

K–45

301 LITTLE
SIOUX

183

NEBRASKA

RIVER SIOUX

N

- 29.4 Straight in the village of Moorhead, where you'll find a cafe, grocery, and convenience store.
- 37.0 Right on County F–20 in the village of Pisgah, where you'll find a cafe, grocery, and convenience store.
- 44.0 Right on Hwy. 301 in the village of Little Sioux, where you'll find a cafe, grocery, and convenience store.
- 45.3 Right on County K–45 in the village of River Sioux. County K-45 becomes 6th St. in Onawa.
- 54.6 Straight on County K–45 in the village of Blencoe, where you'll find a restaurant and a convenience store.
- 58.0 **Caution: Railroad tracks cross K–45 at a sharp angle.**
- 61.3 Left on Hwy. 175 (Iowa St.) in Onawa.
- 61.8 Right on 12th St.
- 62.4 Right to arrive at Gaukel Park.

Michigan

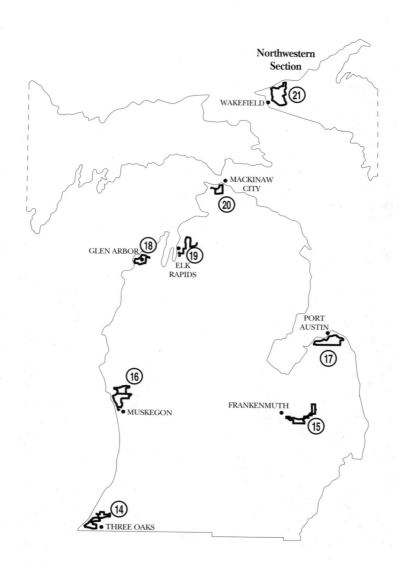

Northwestern Section

WAKEFIELD 21

MACKINAW CITY 20

GLEN ARBOR 18

ELK RAPIDS 19

PORT AUSTIN 17

16 MUSKEGON

FRANKENMUTH 15

14 THREE OAKS

Michigan

14

Apple Cider Cruise

One of the most popular bicycle tours in the country is the annual Apple Cider Century, held the last Sunday in September. The ride explores the shore of Lake Michigan and inland orchards as it guides 7,000 riders on the road to bicycling adventure. It takes 6,000 slices of apple pie and 2,000 gallons of apple cider, along with similar quantities of other foods and more bananas than I like to think about, to keep the Midwest's largest bicycle tour rolling. This loop is one of four included in the event. The others are 25, 75, and 100 miles in length. In its twenty years the Apple Cider Century has grown exponentially, thanks to the small but active membership of the Three Oaks Bicycle Club. A mere 226 rode in the first, in 1974. Today an entry limit is enforced to keep things manageable.

The route rambles, but its heart is at the Bicycle Museum in Three Oaks, which is the starting point for this loop. The museum was made possible by the success of the Apple Cider Century. Inside you can see examples of cycling's relentless technical progress, from the bone shaker and giant highwheeler to today's custom-built racing bike. Posters, equipment, and other memorabilia recall bicycling's turn-of-the-century heyday.

Three Oaks is a quaint old railroad town, with its roots planted firmly in the days of bicycling's infancy. Its big splash in American industry was a booming corset factory that used turkey-feather quills for stays. Ironically, the extreme popularity of the bicycle caused these restrictive garments to go out of fashion. Today the Apple Cider Century's director, Bryan Volstorf, is the mayor of Three Oaks, and the tour is a point of pride in the town. So things have come full circle.

As you pedal over the gently rolling Michigan farmland, you'll ride past Warren Woods State Forest. Edward K. Warren was an early conservationist who bought the land in 1879 to save a beautiful stand of virgin beech-maple trees. Today they stand as a climax forest of giant trees that have never seen an ax or saw.

At the village of New Troy, you'll find the Old Mill Run Mexican Restaurant, a favorite with hungry bicyclists. Beyond the village the route rolls through some of the apple orchards that give the ride its name.

Heading east the route takes a side trip to Warren Dunes State Park. These 4,700 acres on the Lake Michigan shoreline with spectacular sand dunes were also preserved by the foresight of Edward K. Warren. Southeast of the park in Harbert you'll find another popular bicyclist's stop: the Swedish Bakery.

New Buffalo owes its existence to the fickle weather of Lake Michigan. In 1834 the sailing ship *Post Boy,* out of Buffalo, New York, broke up before an autumn storm and was driven onto the sandy shore. Its captain, Wessel Whittaker, eyed the estuary of the Galien River and envisioned another Chicago. Back home he sold investors on the scheme, and the town was born. What nature gives it can also take away, and it was impossible to keep the harbor open with the relentless, wave-driven sands. New Buffalo turned its back on those pretensions and settled for being a railroad and tourist town. On the way out of town, you'll pass the old railroad depot, which today serves as a museum and antiques shop.

The Basics

Start: Park in the parking lot of the Bicycle Museum at 1 Oak St. in Three Oaks.

Length: 57.0 miles.

Terrain: Flat to gently rolling.

Food: There are several restaurants and a grocery in Three Oaks. In New Troy there is a Mexican restaurant. There is a concession stand at Warren Dunes State Park. At Harbert are a restaurant, bakery, and fruit market. In New Buffalo you'll find restaurants, groceries, convenience stores, and ice cream shops.

For more information: Apple Cider Century, P.O. Box 7000, Three Oaks, MI 49128; (616) 756–3361. Harbor Country Chamber of Commerce, 3 W. Buffalo, New Buffalo, MI 49117; (616) 469–5409 or (800) 362–7251.

Bicycle service: In Union Pier.

Miles & Directions

- 0.0 Ride north on Elm St. from the Bicycle Museum.
- 0.9 Left on Kruger Rd.
- 2.9 Right on Basswood Rd.
- 3.7 Left on Union Pier Rd.
- 4.8 Right on Lakeside Rd.
- 5.6 Right on Warren Woods Rd.
- 10.6 Left on Carpenter Rd.
- 11.6 Left on Kaiser Rd.
- 12.3 Right on Minnich Rd.
- 13.4 Right on Hanover Rd.
- 14.3 Left on Mill Rd., which becomes Glendora Rd.
- 14.8 Proceed straight in the village of New Troy, where you'll find a Mexican restaurant.
- 19.8 Left on Hills Rd. (orchards).
- 21.3 Left on Browntown Rd.
- 24.9 Right on Date Rd.
- 26.5 Left on Snow Rd.
- 30.4 Right on Browntown Rd.
- 31.8 Right on Red Arrow Hwy.
- 32.0 Left into Warren Dunes State Park.
- 33.2 Turn around at the park swimming beach, where you'll find a concession stand.
- 34.4 Right on Red Arrow Hwy.
- 34.6 Left on Browntown Rd.
- 35.0 Right on Flynn Rd.
- 37.0 Right on Harbert Rd.
- 39.1 Left on Red Arrow Hwy. in the village of Harbert, where you'll find a restaurant, bakery, and fruit market.

- 40.0 Right on Lake Shore Rd.
- 44.8 Right on Riviera Rd., which becomes Whittaker St. in New Buffalo, where you'll find restaurants, groceries, convenience stores, and ice cream shops.
- 47.9 Proceed straight in New Buffalo across U.S. Hwy. 12 onto Whittaker St., which becomes La Porte Rd.
- 48.4 Left on Jefferson Rd., which becomes Maudlin Rd.
- 52.3 Straight across Lakeside Rd. onto Forest Lawn Rd.
- 55.5 Left on Three Oaks Rd., which becomes Elm St. in Three Oaks.
- 57.0 Arrive at the Bicycle Museum in Three Oaks.

15

Frankenmuth Fahrrad Ramble

In German *fahrrad* means "cycling," and Frankenmuth is nothing if not German. The small town has turned its German heritage into a thriving business. In fact, it's the most popular tourism destination in Michigan. On the third weekend of May you can join the local Optimists Club and 300-plus bicyclists on 25-, 50-, and 100-kilometer routes. That's 16, 31, and 62 miles in non-Euro terms. The 31-mile version was chosen for this book.

Frankenmuth is known as Michigan's "Little Bavaria," and it does its utmost to live up to that description. With everything from onion-domed towers to waiters in lederhosen, the town celebrates its German roots. You'll find shops featuring Old World crafts, baked goods, sausage, and even a brewery that predates the micro-brew craze by 130 years with a selection of rich, frothy beers. Don't expect to pick up a suitcase of cans for a football weekend. The brews are barreled or bottled, strong, and pricey enough to moderate your consumption.

Frankenmuth is famous for its chicken dinners. Two huge restaurants owned by related families, who have been in the business for over a hundred years, serve over two million family-style dinners a year. That's enough chow to handle all the hungry bicyclists in the state.

When you finally tear yourself from Frankenmuth, you'll pedal east through mixed woods and farmland paralleling the meandering Cass River, crossing four tributary streams en route to the quaint farm community of Vassar. Vassar is probably what Frankenmuth would be like without tourism. The towers and spires of Frankenmuth will poke the horizon on your way back. Winding through town, you'll cross a picturesque covered bridge on the way back to Heritage Park.

You might think that neighboring towns would jump on the bandwagon with some ethnic theme or another. Don't look for a European Union in Michigan though. Frankenmuth is one of a kind.

The Basics

Start: Park in Heritage Park 0.3 miles east on Hwy. 83 (Main St.), then north on Weiss St.
Length: 28.7 miles.
Terrain: Flat to gently rolling.
Food: There are restrooms and water in Heritage Park and numerous restaurants, groceries, and fast-food operations in Frankenmuth. In Vassar there is a cafe and grocery.
For more information: Frankenmuth Fahrrad Bike Tour, Optimists Club of Frankenmuth, P.O. Box 335, Frankenmuth, MI 48734. Frankenmuth Convention & Visitors Bureau, 535 S. Main St., Frankenmuth, MI 48734; (517) 652–6106 or (800) FUN TOWN.

Miles & Directions

- 0.0 Ride straight out of Heritage Park onto Weiss St.
- 0.5 Left on E. Jefferson St.
- 1.5 Right on S. Block Rd.
- 2.5 Left on E. Townline Rd., which becomes Swaffer Rd.
- 4.8 Left on Barkley Rd.
- 5.9 Left on Ormes Rd. followed by an immediate right.
- 6.2 Right on Loren Rd.
- 8.1 Left on Buell Rd.
- 9.6 Left on Pinkerton Rd.
- 11.0 Left on Vassar Rd., which becomes Water St. in the town of Vassar where you'll find a cafe and a grocery.
- 12.3 Right on Plumb St.

- 12.4 Left on Hwy. 15 (Goodrich Rd.).
- 12.6 Left on Hwy. 15 (Huron Rd.).
- 12.9 Right on Division St.
- 14.3 Left on Waterman Rd.
- 15.4 Left on Cottrell Rd., which becomes John Rd.
- 20.6 Left on Lorenzo Rd.
- 21.7 Bear right onto Van Cleve Rd. in the village of Tuscola. Van Cleve Rd. becomes Tuscola Rd. and E. Tuscola St. in Frankenmuth.
- 25.5 Right on Cherry St.
- 25.6 Left on E. School St.
- 25.7 Right on Parker St.
- 25.8 Left on E. Genesee St.
- 26.9 Left on Mayer Rd.
- 27.3 Left on W. Tuscola St.
- 27.8 Right on Gunzenhausen St.
- 28.1 Right across Main St. onto Covered Bridge Lane.
- 28.4 Left on Weiss St.
- 28.7 Arrive at Heritage Park.

16

Bike Across Nature's Grandeur Challenge

Acronyms are the rage in the computer age. Words made from initials convey a message that a full name may not. Bicycle across Nature's Grandeur (BANG) gives you the idea that you're in for some great scenery on this tour. BANG lets you know that the organized ride always takes place the first Saturday of July, right around the Fourth. Ride director Arland Cutler and the Muskegon Bicycle Club add some holiday flair by giving each rider a few snappers to liven things up more than the occasional blowout. BANG also includes a 100-mile-route option. To add to the festivities, the Muskegon Summerfest arts and crafts fair is always held on the same weekend.

In 1871 the fireworks were in Chicago. The lumber industry was big in Muskegon, and after the Great Chicago Fire forty-four sawmills ran night and day turning native white pine into lumber for the devastated city across Lake Michigan. Today the mills are gone, but the trees have regrown and BANG will take you through the great stands of the Manistee National Forest. The shore of Lake Michigan and inland lakes are the other attractions for BANG. The forest has come back, and the lakes never lost their charm.

From the starting point, at the boat launch pier at Muskegon State Park, you'll get an eyeful of the scenery BANG is known for. The view is of Muskegon Lake, a rivermouth made into a lake by the huge sandbar you're standing on. Across the channel between Muskegon Lake and Lake Michigan lies the World War II submarine USS *Silversides,* a floating museum. Riding north out of the park, you'll get a taste of Great Lakes scenery before turning east to skirt the shore of Muskegon Lake.

Waves of water soon give way to waves of wheat and corn as you head north and east over the gently rolling farmland. If the heat is getting to you, the Michigan Adventure Amusement Park, with its roller coaster and water park, is at the crossing of Whitehall Road. Going north again on Staples Road, the terrain becomes more varied, and you soon swing east for a scenic loop around West, North, and Twin lakes.

North on Russell Road you pedal through the heart of the Manistee National Forest and follow the transition from white oak to pine and hemlock. After looping around Big Blue Lake, the terrain flattens and you have a chance to pause by the spillway of the small dam across Sand Creek. Farther east you'll cross the Hart-Montague Trail, a 6-foot-wide, 22-mile-long paved bike trail. If you're there in August, the fields along Lamos Road will be covered with bright yellow sunflowers.

The sister towns of Montague and Whitehall lie at the head of White Lake, noted for its sailboat marina and the world's largest weather vane. There's more nautical sightseeing to be enjoyed by taking a 1-mile excursion off the route, where South Shore and Scenic Drive meet, to the White River Lighthouse Museum. The museum is a fully operating lighthouse with artifacts and notes on historic shipwrecks.

Expect a moderate headwind as you pedal south along the Lake Michigan shore. You'll pass two more parks and, just before the end, the biggest hill on the route. Blockhouse Hill rises 150 feet above the level of the lake for a great view and a 40-mile-an-hour downhill run.

The Basics

Start: Muskegon State Park, east of North Muskegon on Memorial Dr.
Length: 49.4 or 66.6 miles.
Terrain: Flat to rolling.
Food: There are many restaurants and stores in Muskegon and North Muskegon. It will be a long distance before your first on-route food option at Nichols Rd. and Fruitvale Rd., where you'll

find the Trading Post, a small grocery. There are several pharmacies with cafes along the route in Montague. There are also several restaurants on Business Hwy. 31 (Water St.), to the left off the route in downtown Montague.

For more information: Muskegon Bicycle Club, Inc., 2722 Memorial Dr., Muskegon, MI 49445; (616) 744–5824. Muskegon County Visitor & Convention Bureau, 610 Western Ave., Muskegon, MI 49440; (800) 250–WAVE; Web site www.muskegon.org.

Bicycle service: One shop in Montague and two in Muskegon.

Miles & Directions

- 0.0 Follow Scenic Dr. from the boat launch parking lot in Muskegon State Park.
- 1.5 Right on Memorial Dr.
- 4.4 Left on Bear Lake Rd.
- 6.0 Right on Fenner Rd.
- 6.3 Left on Horton Rd.
- 8.6 Left on River Rd.
- 9.4 Right on Lorenson Rd..
- 11.9 Right on Duck Lake Rd.
- 12.4 Left on Gibson Rd.
- 12.9 Right on Riley-Thompson Rd.
- 17.5 Left on Staple Rd.
- 19.7 Right on W. Lake Dr.
- 20.7 Left on Middle Lake Dr.
- 21.2 Right on Duff Rd.
- 22.2 Left on Blue Lake Rd.
- 22.7 Left on White Lake Rd.

To complete the shorter 49.4-mile route, continue straight at mile 26.3 at the junction with Russell Rd. At mile 34.6 turn left at S. Shore Dr. At mile 36.2 turn right on S. Shore Dr. From here pick up the directions below at mile 53.4.

- 26.3 Right on Russell Rd.

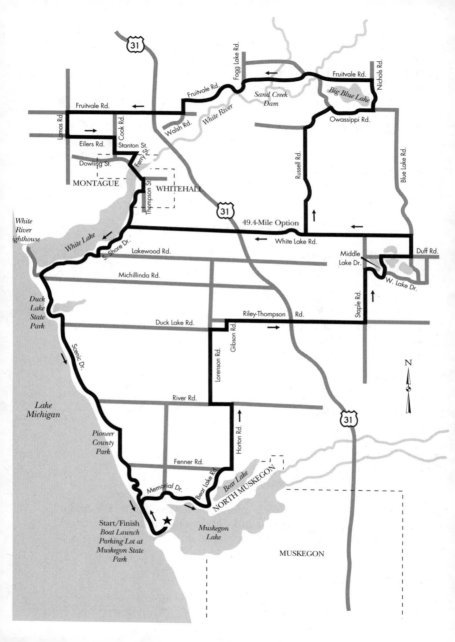

- 31.3 Right on Owassippi Rd.
- 32.7 Left on Nichols Rd.
- 33.8 Left on Fruitvale Rd., where you'll find a small store, the Trading Post, with food and drink.
- 36.0 Bear left at the unmarked intersection, toward Happy Mohawk Canoe Livery; follow the dead-end road.
- 37.3 Walk across the 50-foot-long dam at the road's end. This is a nice resting place.
- 37.8 Straight at Fogg Lake Rd. You're actually continuing on Fruitvale Rd.
- 41.5 Right on Fruitvale Rd. at the intersection with Weesies Rd. and Walsh Rd. Cross the overpass over U.S. Hwy. 31.
- 45.4 Left on Lamos Rd.
- 46.4 Left on Eilers Rd.
- 47.9 Right on Cook Rd. in the outskirts of the town of Montague.
- 48.4 Left on Stanton St.
- 49.1 Right on Ferry St., where you'll find several pharmacies with cafes.
- 49.4 Left on Dowling St. There are several restaurants on Water St., to the left off the route in downtown Montague. You'll cross the neck of White Lake on a causeway with two traffic lanes each way. For a relaxed ride and a leisurely view of the lake, use the bike/walkway along the west side of the causeway.
- 50.0 Right on Thompson St.
- 50.5 Right on S. Shore Dr.
- 53.4 Right on S. Shore Dr. at Lakewood Rd.
- 55.5 Left on Scenic Dr. One mile to the right on Murray Dr. is the White River Lighthouse Museum.
- 55.8 Right on Scenic Dr. at Michillinda Rd.
- 65.1 Proceed straight onto Scenic Dr. and into Muskegon State Park on Memorial Dr.
- 66.6 Arrive at boat launch parking area.

17

Thumbs Up Cruise

Michigan is really two states, a fact not much changed by the building of the great Mackinac Bridge. North of the bridge is the Upper Peninsula, sitting like a cocked hat on the state of Wisconsin. People in the UP are called Yoopers—*U-Pe*rs, get it? The Lower Peninsula, where almost all of the people live, is called the mitten, because it's shaped like a mitten. The rounded peninsula north of Detroit is called the thumb, and that's how the Thumbs Up Bicycle Club and the Thumbs Up Bicycle Tour got their names.

When Tom Morneau bicycled some organized tours in Michigan, he was surprised at how poor the roads were. He thought, "We've got to be able to do better than this. The roads are a lot smoother, and there's no comparison with the scenery." Morneau was involved in two activities that put him in a position to know: He was a bicyclist, and he regularly patrolled the roads for his job as a Huron County deputy sheriff. From such knowledge bike tours are born. The Thumbs Up Bicycle Tour takes place on the second Saturday in June and features four distances, from 12 to 100 miles in length.

Scenery you'll have on this tour. Nearly half of the total distance is along lakeshore. From Port Austin you'll get the first dose as you roll along the flat shoreline of Saginaw Bay. Forests line the inland side of the road, and you'll pass two state parks and a state game area. Expect a seasonal tailwind along this stretch in the spring and a headwind in the summer. There are several swimming beaches along the road, but the best one is at the town park in Caseville. If you think it would be fun to feed the ever-present gulls, be forewarned: "A guy riding with me started feeding gulls and had to leave because of the swarm that came after him," Morneau said.

Turning inland the scenery will change to farmland, with crops of beans, wheat, corn, and barley. Herds of dairy cows dot the farmyards. The little crossroads towns you pass through are there to serve the farmers, and the small cafes have a rural character. In Pinnebog you can get a sandwich at Coon's Farm Market.

As you return to the lakeshore, you'll look out across the vast expanse of Lake Huron, with Canada beyond the horizon. Near Huron City you'll find Lighthouse County Park, which has one of the few hills on the route, and the Pointe aux Barques Light, which warns the Great Lakes freighters to stay clear of the shore. At the Pioneer Huron City Museum, the history of a lifestyle tied to the lake is on display in seven original buildings.

Your last stop on the route is Grind Stone City, where millstones were once quarried. Time seems to have left the town behind, but you'll still find some life at Danny Zebs' restaurant, general store, and ice cream shop. Places like Zebs' are the social centers of rural America.

The Basics

Start: Gallop Park, 1 block south of Hwy. 25 on Sand Rd. in the village of Port Austin, which is at the north end of Hwy. 53.

Length: 61.0 miles.

Terrain: Flat to gently rolling.

Food: There are convenience stores in Port Austin, at several points along Port Austin Rd., in Caseville, and at Gotts Corner. In Pinnebog, Coon's Farm Market serves lunches. There is a cafe in Kinde. In Lewisville there are a convenience store, a cafe, and a tavern. In Grind Stone City you'll find a convenience store and Danny Zebs' restaurant, general store, and ice cream shop.

For more information: Thumbs Up Bicycle Club, 1667 S. Hellems Rd., Bad Axe, MI 48413; Tom and Julie Morneau, (517) 269–7136. Huron County Visitors Bureau, 250 E. Huron, Bad Axe, MI 48413; (507) 269–8463.

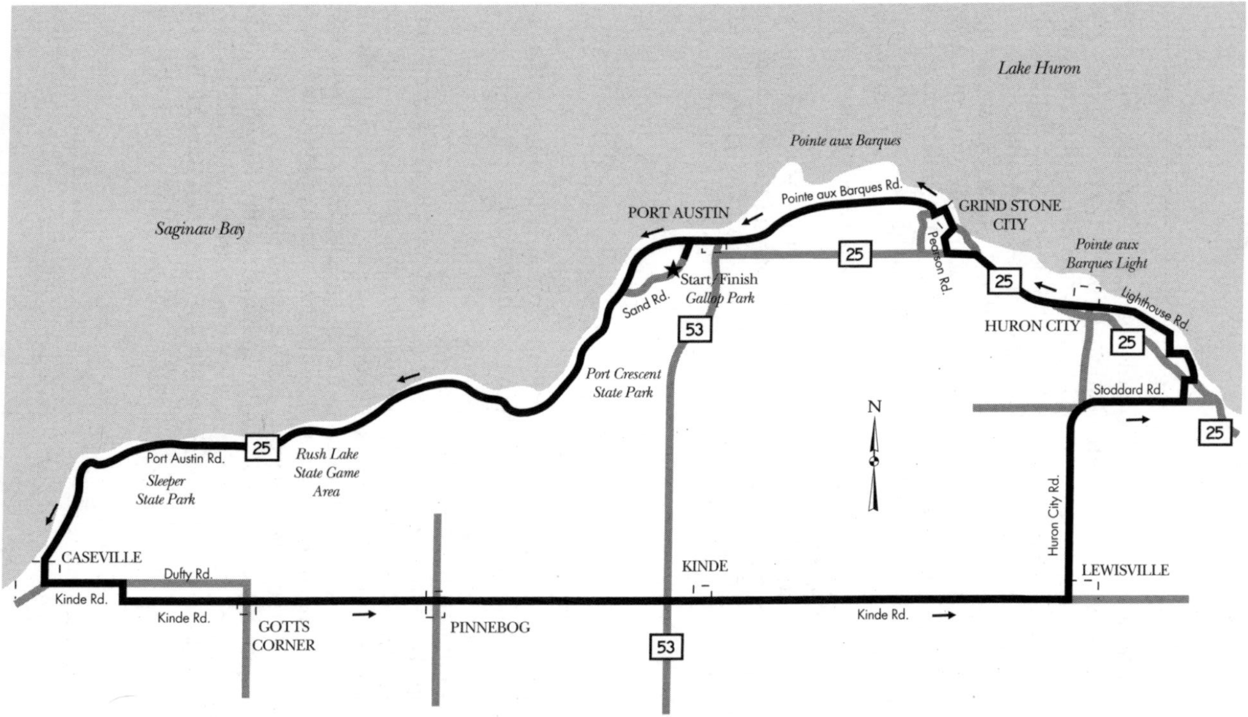

Lake Huron

Saginaw Bay

Pointe aux Barques

Pointe aux Barques Light

GRIND STONE CITY

Pearson Rd.

Pointe aux Barques Rd.

HURON CITY

Lighthouse Rd.

Stoddard Rd.

LEWISVILLE

Huron City Rd.

N

PORT AUSTIN

Start/Finish

Gallup Park

Sand Rd.

Port Crescent State Park

KINDE

Kinde Rd.

PINNEBOG

GOTTS CORNER

CASEVILLE

Port Austin Rd.

Sleeper State Park

Rush Lake State Game Area

Duffy Rd.

Kinde Rd.

Kinde Rd.

25

25

25

25

25

25

53

53

53

Miles & Directions

- 0.0 North on Sand Rd. from Gallop Park.
- 0.1 Left on Hwy. 25 (Port Austin Rd.). **Use caution, and ride on the wide paved shoulder because seasonal traffic may be significant.**
- 4.0 Pass Port Crescent State Park, where you'll find a convenience store.
- 18.0 Left on Kinde Rd. in Caseville, where you'll find a convenience store.
- 19.6 Right on Kinde Rd. at the intersection with Dufty Rd.
- 22.5 Continue straight at Gotts Corner, where you'll find a convenience store.
- 26.6 Continue straight at Pinnebog Rd., where you'll find a store and restaurant.
- 31.5 Straight at Hwy. 53 into the village of Kinde, where you'll find a cafe.
- 40.1 Left on Huron City Rd. in Lewisville, where you'll find a convenience store, a cafe, and a tavern.
- 44.1 Right on Stoddard Rd.
- 46.4 Left on Minden Rd.
- 46.9 Right on Hwy. 25.
- 47.0 Left on Lighthouse Rd.
- 50.4 Straight at Huron City Rd. in Huron City.
- 51.0 Right on Hwy. 25 (Grind Stone Rd.).
- 53.7 Right on Pearson Rd. into the village of Grind Stone City, where you'll find a convenience store and Danny Zebs' restaurant, general store, and ice cream shop.
- 54.9 Right on Pointe aux Barques Rd.
- 60.2 Straight onto Port Austin Rd. at Hwy. 53 in Port Austin.
- 60.9 Left on Sand Rd.
- 61.0 Arrive at Gallop Park.

18

Leelanau Lakeshore Ramble

Ojibwa legend tells of Sleeping Bear, a solitary dune above the Lake Michigan shore. In ancient times a mother bear swam the lake with her two cubs to escape a forest fire. On shore she climbed to a high point to watch for her lost little ones. But the cubs drowned, and now, as she peers eternally to the west, she sees what her offspring became: the Manitou Islands. This tour takes you through the magical landscape of Sleeping Bear Dunes National Lakeshore. It's one of the routes on the three-day Leelanau Lakeshore Loop, organized by the American Lung Association of Michigan and held the second weekend of September. Each day different tours of 30 or 50 miles are offered.

A place has to be pretty extraordinary to be designated a national lakeshore, and that description fits Sleeping Bear Dunes perfectly. The 300- to 400-foot-high dunes are the gift of the last continental glacier that filled the Lake Michigan basin as recently as 12,000 years ago. Pushing southward it pulverized soft sedimentary rock, making perfect dune material: sand. As glacial ice melted, the lake level was often higher than it is today. A prevailing westerly wind was the final ingredient needed to relentlessly pile grain on grain, year after year, until towering dunes remained.

The constant, drifting sands cut off bays, and inland lakes formed. As the dunes age, grasses and trees stabilize the sand and they look little different from other wooded hills. At Sleeping Bear Point, though, the dunes are bare. Shifting sands, landslides, and blowouts can change the landscape in the blink of a geologic eye. Here and there the sand shifts to reveal a ghost forest of standing trees that were once engulfed by the same forces that finally exposed them.

The ride begins at Sugar Loaf Resort, where in winter a huge dune becomes a ski hill. It's an easy roll down to Highway 22, which winds between the massive dunes held in place by the roots of grasses and trees. At Glen Arbor you'll ride on the lake side of the dunes, and if the wind is strong from the northwest, you'll feel its force as you watch angry whitecaps roll into Sleeping Bear Bay. A few miles farther, as you skirt the west edge of Glen Lake, you can leave your bike and hike up Dune Climb Trail to see things from the perspective of the ever-present gulls. If you don't mind adding seven hilly miles to your ride, you can take the Pierce Stocking Scenic Drive, just south of Hariger Road on Route 109.

The Basics

Start: Sugar Loaf Resort, just off of Hwy. 22 or County 615, 6 miles north of the town of Cedar.
Length: 33.4 miles.
Terrain: Flat, rolling, and hilly.
Food: There are several restaurants at Sugar Loaf Resort. In Glen Arbor you'll find restaurants, a grocery, and a convenience store. There is an ice cream shop in Burdickville.
For more information: American Lung Association of Michigan, 29 Pearl St., Suite 305, Grand Rapids, MI 49503; (800) 263–5880. Traverse City Area Chamber of Commerce, P.O. Box 387, Traverse City, MI 49685-0387; (616) 947–5075.
Bicycle service: In nearby Traverse City.

Miles & Directions

- 0.0 Ride north, downhill on Sugar Loaf Mountain Rd.
- 0.8 Left on Hwy. 22. **Caution: Ride on the paved shoulder because significant traffic may be encountered.**
- 10.9 Continue straight in the village of Glen Arbor, where you'll find restaurants, a grocery, and a convenience store.
- 11.3 Straight on Hwy. 109 when Hwy. 22 turns left.
- 13.3 Left on Hwy. 109.

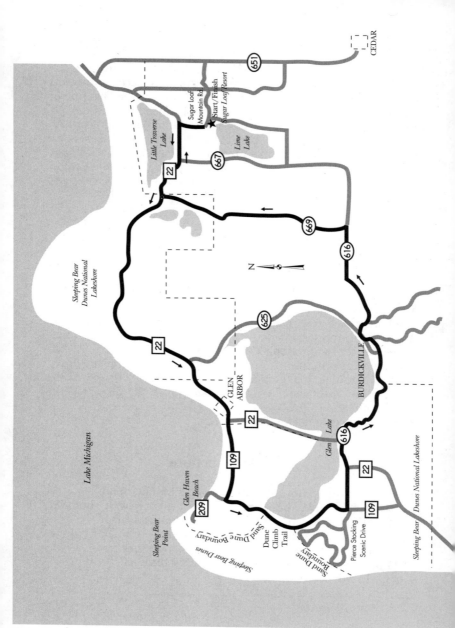

- 14.8 Dune Climb Trail with scenic view is on the right.
- 16.3 Left on County 616 (W. Hariger Rd.).
- 17.7 Bear left on Hwy. 22 (S. Leelanau).
- 18.5 Straight on County 616 when Hwy. 22 turns left.
- 20.1 Inspiration Point overlooks Glen Lake at the top of a climb.
- 20.8 Straight on County 616.
- 22.1 Right on County 616 in Burdickville, where you'll find an ice cream shop.
- 25.0 Left on County 669.
- 29.7 Right on Hwy. 22.
- 32.6 Right on Sugar Loaf Mountain Rd.
- 33.4 Arrive at Sugar Loaf Resort.

19

Cherry Blossom Cruise

If ever there was proof positive of the ability of nature's beauty to buoy the human spirit, it's during blossom time in spring. On the hills overlooking Grand Traverse Bay, this is when the orchards are blankets of pink cherry blossoms. The peak comes in mid-May, and on the third weekend of the month the Northwest Michigan Child Guidance Center hosts its annual Cherry Blossom Pedal Bike Tour, with routes of 15, 50, and 72 miles.

In the days when it was a port for transshipping lumber and iron, Elk Rapids was larger than nearby Traverse City, but you'll be glad that time passed it by and left the surroundings free from sprawl. Its natural harbor is a perfect spot for the Municipal Park, with its swimming beach and picnic area. From there the route heads south of town to the 200-foot orchard-covered hills and views of Grand Traverse Bay to the west and Elk Lake to the east.

Near the southern end of the route, you have the choice of visiting the Grand Traverse Resort or Amon's Orchard. You can see the glass tower of the resort for a long distance. It's known for its Jack Nicklaus–designed golf course and the overlook from the seventeen-story tower. You can enjoy the view by taking a lunch break at the Trillium restaurant on the top floor. Amon's Orchard is a different experience. It's a farm market with a bakery and has cherries, apples, and peaches in season. It also offers free hayrides and a petting zoo with farm animals.

Cherries are big business, as the acreage devoted to them hints. A thousand tons from a single orchard is not unheard of. The business was revolutionized in the 1960s by a machine that shakes each tree, bringing all the cherries down in just a minute or so. Before they were all picked by hand.

Back in Elk Rapids you may want to check out the Harbor Cafe or Zagger's Market on River Street. North of town the route covers more orchard country while taking in a closer look at the blue, clear Lake Michigan waters. On North Bay Shore Road, you'll have great views of the bay, with its sandy beaches, woods, and occasional cottages. As you near the inland lakes, you may spot blue herons, Canada geese, bald eagles, and swans.

Along Torch Lake you'll ride past a wooded shoreline with occasional views of the 250-foot-deep glacial lake where windsurfing and boating are popular summer pastimes. At the turnaround point in the village of Alden, you can take a break overlooking the lake at the Spencer Creek Cafe, known for its soups and lunches. And no matter where you stop, you can expect to see cherry this and cherry that on the dessert menu.

The Basics

Start: Park on River St. across from Elk Rapids Municipal Park and begin riding at the intersection of Pine St.
Length: 56.9 miles.
Terrain: Hilly to gently rolling.
Food: There are numerous restaurants in Elk Rapids, as well as a grocery and an ice cream shop. Amon's Orchard has a bakery and sells seasonal fruits at a farm market. There are several restaurants at Grand Traverse Resort. In Kewadin are a convenience store with deli sandwiches and a bar that serves burgers. There is a restaurant in Torch River. In Alden there are several restaurants and a bakery.
For more information: Cherry Blossom Pedal Bike Tour, Child Guidance Center, Inc., 1100 Silver Dr., Suite C, Traverse City, MI 49684; (616) 947–2255. Traverse City Area Chamber of Commerce, P.O. Box 387, Traverse City, MI 49685-0387; (616) 947–5075.
Bicycle service: In nearby Traverse City.

Miles & Directions

- 0.0 Ride east on River St. from the intersection of Pine St.

- 0.4 Right on U.S. Hwy. 31. **Caution: Significant traffic may be encountered.**
- 1.1 Left on County 605 (Elm Lake Rd.).
- 5.2 Right on Angell Rd.
- 6.7 Left on Bates Rd.
- 7.7 Right on Yuba Rd.
- 8.1 Left on Sayler Rd.
- 10.1 Right on Brackett Rd.
- 11.6 Left on Lautner Rd.

*If you wish to visit Amon's Orchard, continue straight on Brackett Rd. and turn right on U.S. Hwy. 31 at mile 12.0. **Use caution and ride on the paved shoulder until mile 12.6,** when you'll be at the roadside orchard market. Return by the same route and pick up directions below at mile 14.1.*

- 12.3 Right into Grand Traverse Resort.
- 12.7 Turn around at Grand Traverse Resort, where you'll find several restaurants.
- 13.3 Left on Lautner Rd.
- 14.1 Right on Brackett Rd.
- 16.1 Left on Bates Rd.
- 19.0 Right on Angell Rd.
- 20.5 Left on County 605.
- 24.5 Right on U.S. Hwy. 31.
- 25.9 Left on N. Bay Shore Rd. in Elk River.
- 28.2 Straight across U.S. Hwy. 31 onto Williams Rd.
- 29.2 Left on Cairn Hwy.
- 29.4 Right on County 593 (Cherry Ave.).
- 29.8 Continue straight in the village of Kewadin, where you'll find a convenience store and a tavern.
- 31.2 Left on Bussa Rd.
- 32.1 Right on Western Rd.
- 34.4 Left on Hicken Rd.
- 34.9 Right on W. Shore Dr.
- 37.0 Left on County 593 (Crystal Beach Rd.).
- 40.9 Turn around in the village of Alden, where you'll find several restaurants and a bakery.

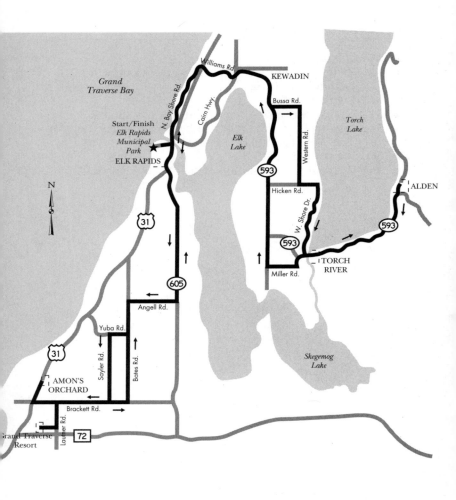

- 44.9 Left on Miller Rd.
- 46.1 Right on Cherry Ave., which becomes County 593.
- 52.7 Left on Cairn Hwy.
- 52.9 Right on Williams Rd.
- 54.0 Straight across U.S. Hwy. 31 onto N. Bay Shore Rd.
- 56.2 Left on Dexter St., followed by an immediate right onto U.S. Hwy. 31 in Elk Rapids.
- 56.5 Right on River St.
- 56.9 Arrive at the intersection of River St. and Pine St.

20

Big Mac Shoreline Ramble

"Big Mac" is the Mackinac Bridge, which connects upper and lower Michigan. The towering structure is one of the world's greatest bridges. Completed in 1957, it put a road over the crossroads of the Great Lakes. The straits are where Lake Michigan and Lake Huron meet and near where the St. Mary River pours forth the waters of Lake Superior. In the past the straits were a key point for trade and defense. Today tourism draws people to the straits, including hundreds of bicyclists who ride the 100-, 75-, 50-, and 25-mile routes of the Big Mac Shoreline Scenic Bike Tour on the second weekend of June and September.

The starting point is near the log palisade of restored Fort Michilimackinac, site of one of the most dramatic conflicts in our history. Built by the French, it was ceded to the British in 1763. A stroke of the pen on the Treaty of Ghent relinquished all French claim to Canada and the Great Lakes. It ended a global conflict that was known in North America as the French and Indian War.

The tribes of Native Americans didn't accept British rule easily. To their mind they'd won great victories for the French in the wilderness and now were forced to deal with Redcoats who lacked the French traders' understanding of their customs. An Ottawa chief named Pontiac secretly conspired with tribes throughout the Great Lakes to drive out the British.

At Fort Michilimackinac the attack was particularly crafty. An intense game of lacrosse was under way between the Ojibwa and Sauk beneath the fort walls. Redcoats were betting heavily on the rivals as they watched from the palisade. Suddenly, the ball was hurled into the fort. To keep the game from coming to a halt, the soldiers opened the gate. As the players rushed in, they grabbed tomahawks from women who'd hidden them under their blankets. Within minutes the garrison was wiped out.

Pontiac's uprising failed, although eight of the twelve forts the conspirators attacked fell. The British returned and eventually built a stronger fort on nearby Mackinac Island. They learned to deal more fairly with the tribes, and by the War of 1812 most tribes sided with them.

On the Sunday after the Big Mac Shoreline Scenic Bike Tour, the organizers stage a mass ride across the bridge, which, as an inter-state highway, is normally closed to bike traffic. Once on the north-ern side, riders have the option of returning on the bridge or riding a ferry to Mackinac Island. The island is motor-vehicle-free, and all transport is horse-drawn or by foot or bicycle. A flat, 8-mile paved road circles the island, and a few paved and numerous gravel roads go up the steep slopes, where you can explore the island's interior.

If you're a history buff, the island's fort and other historic sites are as interesting as Fort Michilimackinac at Mackinaw City. At ei-ther location you have to try one of the many restaurants where fresh Great Lakes whitefish is the main fare. It's a short time from lake to plate in this area where commercial fishing boats still ply the waters each day.

Out in the country southwest of Mackinaw City, you'll pedal easily along the lakeshore and over the flat farmland. The side trip to Wilderness State Park is a real treat. The park has 9,000 acres of pine, spruce, tamarack, and cedar on a peninsula containing the longest stretch of public beach and shoreline in the state. The beaches vary in character, and the park is a beachcomber's delight. The best swimming beach is on Big Stone Bay, across from the park campground. On your ride back out Wilderness Park Drive, you'll have a magnificent view of the Mackinac Bridge beyond the light-house on McGulpin Point.

The Basics

Start: Park on the street in front of the Fort Restaurant on Lou-vingny St.

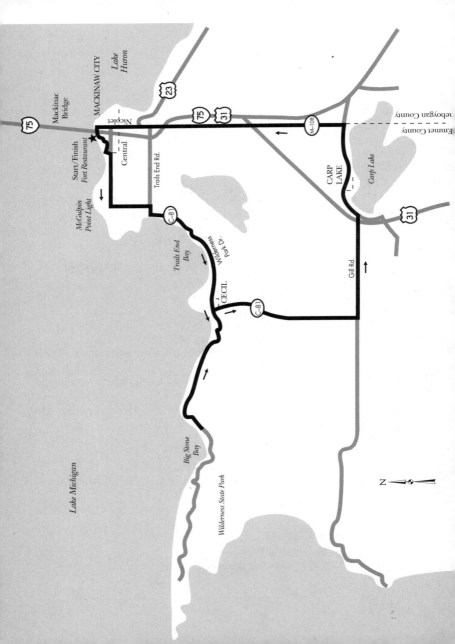

Length: 29.1 miles.

Terrain: Flat.

Food: Numerous restaurants, groceries, and fudge and ice cream shops in Mackinaw City; a convenience store in Cecil; and a convenience store and tavern in Carp Lake.

For more information: Mackinaw Area Tourist Bureau, 708 S. Huron Ave., P.O. Box 160, Mackinaw City, MI 49701; (616) 436–5664 or (800) 666–0160. Mackinac Island State Park Commission, Mackinac Island, MI 49757; (906) 847–3328.

Bicycle service: In Mackinaw City and Mackinac Island.

Miles & Directions

- 0.0 Ride south on Louvingny St. from the Fort Restaurant.
- 0.1 Right on Sinclair St.
- 0.2 Left on Straits St.
- 0.4 Right on Lakeside St.
- 0.6 Right on Central St., which becomes C–81.
- 1.9 Left on C–81 at the T intersection.
- 2.9 Right on Wilderness Park Dr. at the intersection with Trails End Rd.
- 6.5 Straight on Wilderness Park Dr. at Cecil, where you'll find a convenience store.
- 10.3 Turn around at Big Stone Bay picnic area in Wilderness State Park.
- 14.1 Right on C–81 (Cecil Bay Rd.).
- 17.7 Left on Gill Rd.
- 20.3 Straight across U.S. Hwy. 31 onto Gill Rd.
- 21.2 Continue straight in the village of Carp Lake, where you'll find a convenience store and a tavern.
- 22.9 Left on M–108, which becomes Nicolet St. in Mackinaw City.
- 28.9 Left on Huron St.
- 29.0 Left on Louvingny St.
- 29.1 Arrive at the Fort Restaurant.

21

North Country Classic

Each year on the fourth weekend of July, a unique century ride attracts people to one of the wildest areas of the Midwest. The North Country Century covers a vast land, ranging from the shores of Lake Superior to the semimountainous wooded inland. You'll be pleasantly surprised to see the lodging and eating options in some of the towns. This is "Big Snow Country," a skier's paradise that gets more than 200 inches of snowfall a year. The extensive services available are one of the reasons the Wakefield Chamber of Commerce sponsors the North Country Century: to get more people to visit this incredible land during the summer and fall. The tour also includes 30-mile and 100-kilometer routes.

The Upper Peninsula of Michigan is a wild and wooded place that the locals call "the last frontier." The popular band in the area is the Yoopers, the nickname for all Upper Peninsula residents—UP, Yoo-Pee, Yooper. The Yoopers's tune "The Second Week of Deer Camp" is especially popular during hunting season, but you're likely to hear one of their songs on the radio any time of the year. If you don't think the things they sing about are funny, you probably wouldn't last long living in the UP.

The view along U.S. Highway 2 will convince you that the UP is nothing if not beautiful. The tumultuous hills to the left are the Gogebic Range, the resistant heart of ancient mountains that once were as high as the Alps. The roll along the shore of Lake Gogebic brings the shimmering blue of the UP's largest lake into the mix of woods and sky.

North of Bergland you'll weave through more wooded hills before beginning a gradual, rolling descent to Lake Superior. Along the way you'll pass a shopping mall. That's right, a shopping mall. It's there because of the White Pine Mine, one of the last copper mines in the UP. Mining copper and iron from this ancient slice of the earth's crust was the lifeblood of the UP from the midnineteenth to the midtwentieth century. The tradition goes back much further. Beginning around 3000 B.C. Native Americans began mining the peninsula's pure copper and hammering and hardening it into weapons and implements. Known as the Copper Culture, it's among the oldest examples of metallurgy in the world.

From Silver Bay you'll roll along the shore of Lake Superior for 3 miles before turning inland at the entrance to Porcupine Mountains Wilderness State Park, 63,000 acres of virgin timber. An interpretive center at the entrance is worth a visit. From there you'll begin a 20-mile-long, gradual climb that will take you 1,100 feet above the level of the lake as you loop around the backside of the "Porkies," as the locals call these mountains. In several spots you'll catch a glimpse of the giant ski jump at Copper Peak, 15 miles to the southeast. It's the only "ski-flying" hill in this hemisphere.

If you haven't been there before, the vastness of the forest and the sparse population are a bit hard to get used to. Your chances of seeing fox, coyote, bear, deer, raccoon, and porcupine are good, and one thing is certain: The UP has the most waterfalls per capita of any place in the United States. There are at least 114, and two, Manabezho and Manido, are very close to the route and readily accessible by foot at Presque Isle State Park. Waterfalls come in all shapes and sizes. When you've seen one, you can't say you've seen them all. Each has its own personality, and it's hypnotizing to watch the water as it spills over, always changing, yet always the same.

The Basics

Start: Park at Eddy Park on the north side of Sunday Lake.
Length: 101.2 miles.
Terrain: Rolling to hilly, with a gradual 1,100-foot climb and descent.
Food: There are several restaurants, groceries, and convenience stores in Wakefield. At the intersection of U.S. Hwy. 2 and County 523, there is a gas station/convenience store. This is just 1 mile

north of the village of Marenisco, which has a restaurant and a grocery. Along Lake Gogebic you'll see a number of resorts that have soft drink machines and small convenience stores. At Merriweather there is a convenience store. In Bergland you'll find restaurants, groceries, and convenience stores. There is a shopping mall with restaurants along Hwy. 64 at White Pine Mine. In Silver City you'll find restaurants, a grocery, and convenience stores. There is a convenience store and an ice cream shop near the entrance to Porcupine Mountains Wilderness State Park. Beyond that you won't find anything until you get back to Wakefield.

For more information: North Country Century Ride, Wakefield Chamber of Commerce, P.O. Box 93, Wakefield, MI 49968; (906) 224-9561.

Bicycle service: In Wakefield.

Miles & Directions

- 0.0 Ride east on the road in Eddy Park.
- 0.3 Right on Chicago Mine Rd.; then make another immediate right on Hwy. 28.
- 1.4 Left on U.S. Hwy. 2. **Use caution, and ride on the wide paved shoulder because significant traffic may be encountered.** Gas station/convenience store at intersection with County 523 to Marenisco.
- 17.1 Left on Hwy. 64. (Resorts along route have vending machines or convenience stores.)
- 35.0 Right on Hwy. 64/28. **Use caution and ride on the paved shoulder.**
- 35.7 Proceed straight in the village of Merriweather, where you'll find a convenience store.
- 39.4 Left on Hwy. 64 in the village of Bergland, where you'll find restaurants, groceries, and convenience stores.
- 57.1 Left on Hwy. 107 at the village of Silver City, where you'll find restaurants, a grocery, and convenience stores.
- 59.8 Left on S. Boundary Rd., where you'll find a convenience store and an ice cream shop.

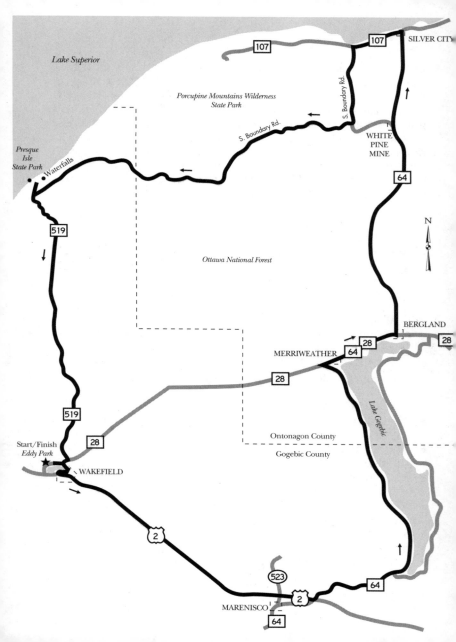

- 64.1 Right on S. Boundary Rd.
- 83.7 Right on Hwy. 519.
- 84.5 Turn around at Presque Isle State Park campground. Continue on Hwy. 519.
- 100.5 Right on Hwy. 28.
- 100.9 Right on Chicago Mine Rd.
- 101.2 Arrive at Eddy Park.

Minnesota

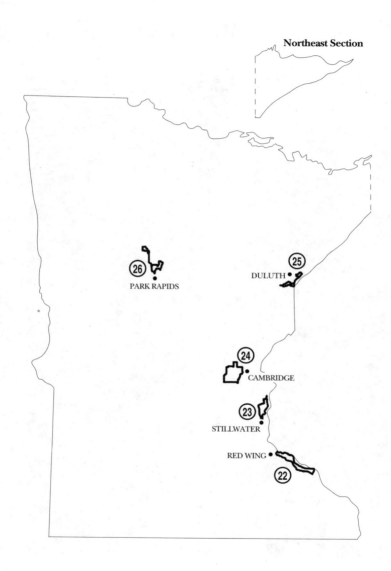

Northeast Section

㉖ PARK RAPIDS

㉕ DULUTH

㉔ CAMBRIDGE

㉓ STILLWATER

RED WING

㉒

Minnesota

22

Lake Pepin Challenge

The Mississippi River is the water highway of America's heartland. It's seldom more scenic than along a 23-mile stretch called Lake Pepin. The delta of the Chippewa River at the south end backs up the water of the Mississippi until it fills the broad width of its valley. Towering limestone bluffs on the Wisconsin side reminded early French explorers of ruined castles.

A circuit of Lake Pepin is an exhilarating mix of flat, rolling, and steep riding, punctuated by beautiful overviews, historic sites, and quaint small towns. Though no longer a part of an organized bike tour, the route is too good to miss. Visitors from the early French to Henry David Thoreau agreed that Lake Pepin is the most scenic stretch of the Mississippi.

The tour begins in Red Wing, Minnesota, a town rich in Victorian architecture and history. It's named after Chief Red Wing and was the ancestral home of the Dakota Sioux. A few pedal strokes take you out of town and out of state. Just over the Mississippi River bridge, you're in Wisconsin, warming up with 7 miles of flat riding. Along the way you'll pass a historical marker for the Bow and Arrow, a rare outline of stones in the form of a drawn bow that's laid out on the side of a steep bluff.

Just after the tiny village of Bay City is a 2.5-mile, 450-foot climb up Oak Ridge. At the top you'll find the picturesque Mt. Tabor Church. The descent brings the first of many great views of Lake Pepin. South of the town of Maiden Rock, the terrain rolls as you skirt the edge of towering limestone palisades. A historical marker notes the Dakota tale about Maiden Rock, wherein a young woman named Wenonah threw herself from the blufftop to avoid marrying a man she didn't love.

Stockholm is an artist's community, with a terrific little restaurant and bakery called the Jenny Lind Cafe, ½ block off the route on County J. Stockholm also has a town park by the lakeshore where a popular art fair is held each year in mid-July. The terrain flattens south of town, and you pass the historical marker for Fort St. Antoine. When the French built the fort in 1686, they celebrated with a display of Chinese fireworks, to the amazement of the Native Americans.

In Pepin you'll find a historical marker for the nearby birthplace of author Laura Ingalls Wilder. Her first book, *Little House in the Big Woods,* recounts her childhood memories of the area. If the village of Nelson is famous for anything, it's got to be for the Nelson Cheese Factory, where you'll find great deals on cheese and generous scoops of ice cream.

Crossing the Mississippi again to return to Minnesota, the route just skirts the town of Wabasha before its junction with U.S. Highway 61, your route for the rest of the tour. Lake City is strung out for several miles along the Lake Pepin shore. North of town the route veers away from the lake, following an old rivercourse between steep bluffs. A few miles later you're back in Red Wing.

The Basics

Start: Broad St. and Levee St. at the Red Wing Depot & Chamber of Commerce in Levee Park, 1 block north of U.S. Hwy. 61 (Main St.), in downtown Red Wing.

Length: 71.2 miles.

Terrain: Flat to rolling, with one long climb.

Food: Red Wing offers the greatest choice of restaurants and fast-food shops. In Bay City there is a tavern and a grocery. You'll find a convenience store and taverns in Maiden Rock. In Stockholm there are cafes, a bakery, and a tavern; the Jenny Lind Cafe is exceptional. Just before entering Pepin you'll see the sign for the Harbor View Cafe, an outstanding eatery. Pepin also has taverns and a grocery. In Nelson there are taverns, a grocery, and the Nelson Cheese Factory, 2 blocks off the route on Hwy. 35. There are restaurants and groceries in Wabasha. In Lake City there are restaurants, groceries, and a Dairy Queen. You'll find a cafe and grocery in Frontenac. Taverns may provide food, from snacks to short-order menus.

For more information: Red Wing Area Chamber of Commerce, 420 Levee St., Red Wing, MN 55066; (612) 388–4719. Mississippi Valley Partners, Box 334, Pepin, WI 54759.

Bicycle service: In Red Wing.

Miles & Directions

- 0.0 Ride 1 block east on Levee Rd.
- 0.1 Right on Bush St.
- 0.2 Straight across U.S. Hwy. 61 (Main St.).
- 0.3 Left on 3rd St.; signs direct you to Wisconsin, north on U.S. Hwy. 63. (The route has a paved shoulder along most of its distance; it allows comfortable riding in traffic that often includes recreational vehicles.)
- 3.3 Right on Hwy. 35.
- 7.4 Continue straight on Hwy. 35 in the village of Bay City, where you'll find a tavern and grocery.
- 15.8 Continue straight in the village of Maiden Rock, where you'll find a convenience store and taverns.
- 22.1 Proceed straight in the village of Stockholm, where you'll find cafes, a bakery, and a tavern.
- 28.4 Continue straight on Hwy. 35 in the village of Pepin, where you'll find a cafe, taverns, and a grocery.
- 32.3 Continue straight across the Chippewa River Bridge.
- 36.6 Straight onto Hwy. 25 in the village of Nelson, where you'll find taverns, a grocery, and the Nelson Cheese Factory, 2 blocks off the route on Hwy. 35.
- 38.9 Continue straight on Hwy. 25 across the Mississippi River Bridge.
- 39.6 Right at the T intersection on County 59 (5th Grant Blvd.) in the town of Wabasha, where you'll find restaurants and groceries.
- 41.1 **Use caution at the rough railroad tracks.**

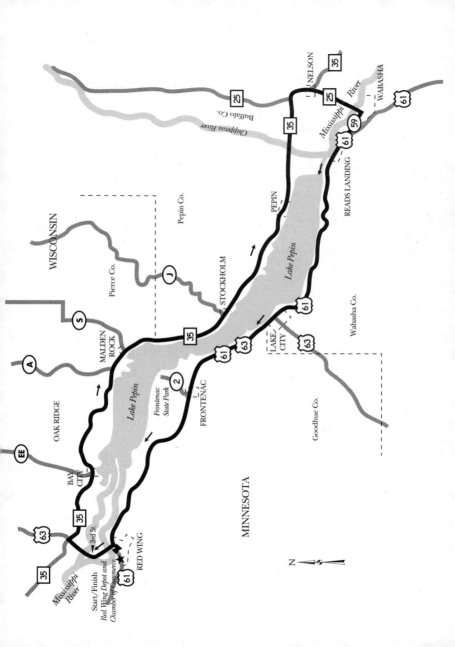

- 41.2 Right on Hwy. 61.
- 52.1 Continue straight in the town of Lake City, where you'll find restaurants, groceries, and a Dairy Queen.
- 60.5 Continue straight on U.S. Hwy. 61/63 in the village of Frontenac, where you'll find a cafe and grocery.
- 69.1 Continue straight on U.S. Hwy. 61 (Main St.) into Red Wing.
- 71.0 Right on Bush St. at the St. James Hotel.
- 71.1 Left at Levee St.
- 71.2 Arrive at the Red Wing Depot & Chamber of Commerce.

23

Fall Colors Ramble

Each autumn the valley of the St. Croix River becomes a mural of brilliant color. This is the time of year several hundred cyclists help the Leukemia Society raise funds by riding the Fall Colors Bike Tour. Starting in the picture-postcard river town of Stillwater, the tour includes a 55-mile route as well as the 25-mile loop described here.

The ride's starting point, in Pioneer Park, offers a gorgeous overview of Stillwater and the St. Croix. The town attracts throngs of visitors to its picturesque setting. Stately Victorian and Greek Revival homes dot the steep hills along the river. In the last century, when the river wasn't jammed with logs waiting to feed the town's sawmills, steamboats plied the waters of the St. Croix. A logjam on the St. Croix once lasted nearly two months and took dynamite to break.

Good food is a big part of the attraction of Stillwater and there are plenty of restaurants to choose from. Check out Vittorio's in the old Wolff Brewery building. The restrooms are in caves once used to cool barrels of beer.

The river is protected along many stretches as part of the St. Croix National Scenic Riverway. Over 250 miles are included north of its confluence with the Mississippi. Near Stillwater the river fills the valley from bluff to bluff. In the fall, the mix of pines and hardwoods make for vibrant contrasts of color on the 300 foot bluffs.

Riding north from Stillwater you'll have a mostly gradual climb to the blufftop. A scenic overlook of the St. Croix along the way is a good spot for a hill-climbing break on your way to the village of Marine on St. Croix, a crossroads town that maintains the character of a bygone time. The general store was the convenience store of the last century and it's still the convenience store in Marine on St. Croix today.

The steepest climb on the route comes as you turn up Nason Hill Road after leaving Marine on St. Croix. You'll make it up 300 feet in 0.5 mile. That's enough bluff for anyone. Once out of the St. Croix Valley, you'll ride through a mix of farm and woodland. The County Park at Square Lake is a great spot to take a break.

The Basics

Start: Park at Pioneer Park, 1 block west of the Hwy. 95 and Hwy. 35 intersection (Water St. and Chestnut St. in downtown Stillwater) on Chestnut St., then bike 4 blocks north on N. 2nd St., where you will find restrooms, water, and a picnic area overlooking the St. Croix and Stillwater.
Length: 25.2 miles.
Terrain: Hilly to gently rolling.
Food: Stillwater has a wide variety of unique restaurants and cafes downtown. In Marine on St. Croix you'll find a general store, tavern, and ice cream shop.
For more information: Fall Colors Bike Tour, Leukemia Society of America, Minnesota Chapter, 5217 Wayzata Blvd., Suite 221, Minneapolis, MN 55416; (612) 545–3309. Stillwater Area Chamber of Commerce, Brick Alley Building, 423 S. Main St., Stillwater, MN 55082; (612) 439–7700.
Bicycle service: In Stillwater.

Miles & Directions

- 0.0 Turn left out of Pioneer Park parking lot and ride south on N. 2nd St. **Caution: steep downhill**.
- 0.3 Left on Myrtle St.
- 0.4 Left on Hwy. 95 (N. Main St.).
- 2.7 Straight at scenic overlook on the St. Croix River.
- 3.1 Straight at wayside rest stop, where you'll find water and restrooms.
- 11.1 Right on County 7 (Judd St.) into the village of Marine on

St. Croix, where you'll find a general store, tavern, and ice cream shop.

- 11.8 Left on Maple St. at the village square followed by a left a ½ block later on Hwy. 95 (St. Croix Tr. N.).
- 12.5 Right on County 7 (Nason Hill Rd.).
- 14.1 Left on County 7 (Paul Ave. N.).
- 15.7 Right on County 7 (Square Lake Rd.) followed by an immediate right into Square Lake County Park, where you'll find restrooms, water, and a swimming beach.
- 15.9 Turn around to return to park entrance.
- 16.0 Right on County 7 (Square Lake Rd.).
- 18.4 Straight on County 55 and County 7 (Norrell Ave. N.).
- 19.0 Left on County 55 (Norrell Ave. N.) where County 7 (Square Lake Rd.) continues straight.
- 20.2 Straight at Pine Point County Park, where you'll find restrooms and water,
- 23.3 Straight across Hwy. 96 (Dellwood Rd.) onto N. Owens St. into Stillwater.
- 24.8 Left on Laurel St. at bottom of steep hill.
- 25.2 Right on N. 2nd St. followed by an immediate left to arrive back at Pioneer Park.

24

Rum River Cruise

The marshes and forests of central Minnesota's Isanti County form the scenic backdrop for the annual Rum River Classic. Three bicycle tour routes are planned. There are 15- and 25-mile loops in addition to the one described here. At the same time the tours are in progress, criterium lap races are held in Cambridge. The events are regularly scheduled on the third weekend in June in conjunction with the town's Swedish/Heritage Festival.

Isanti County is home to the largest concentration of people of Swedish heritage of any county in the United States. The Homestead Act of 1862 opened up the frontier to tides of immigrants, and the Swedes flocked to Minnesota. The Swedish/Heritage Festival celebrates this history with five days of activities featuring a Swedish concert, style show, church service, King's Supper, and folk dancing, including a Maypole Dance. Other aspects are more typically American—a parade, barbecue chicken dinner, country and western music, and, of course, bicycling.

You may notice bumper stickers that state WHEN LUTEFISK IS OUT-LAWED, ONLY OUTLAWS WILL EAT LUTEFISK. They refer to a Scandinavian ritual of preparing and eating fish preserved with lye. It's hard to say which is worse, the cooking or the consuming, but, fortunately, this homage to Norse roots is usually confined to church suppers, and lutefisk won't be found in local restaurants.

Riding north from Cambridge you'll enter a land of woods, marshes, and farmland. Dairy farming is most commonly marked by the signature black-and-white Holstein cows. In the Springvale area the stands of maple trees are particularly beautiful. Such woodlots are home to deer, raccoons, bears, and coyotes. Herons, ducks, and pheasants are seen around the marshlands.

All the roads are in excellent shape, and, with the exception of a

0.5-mile stretch on Highway 47, you may cover the entire route and encounter only a handful of motor vehicles. It's the little things, like songbirds darting from tree to tree, that people appreciate about the central Minnesota countryside, and the speed of a bicycle is perfect for enjoying it all.

The Basics

Start: Park at East Park, at the east side of the Rum River on 2nd Ave. SW, 1 block south of Hwy. 95.

Length: 46.1 miles.

Terrain: Flat to gently rolling.

Food: There are numerous food options in Cambridge. At Springvale Campground, just north of the junction of County 6 and County 14, there is food service at the campground lodge. Otherwise stock up, because you won't find any roadside stores or restaurants on the route.

For more information: Rum River Bicycle Classic, Cambridge Medical Center, 701 S. Dellwood, Cambridge, MN 55008; (612) 689–7700. Cambridge Chamber of Commerce, P.O. Box 343, 238 S. Main St., Cambridge, MN 55008; (612) 689–2505.

Bicycle service: In Cambridge.

Miles & Directions

- 0.0 Head east from the park on 2nd Ave. SW.
- 0.3 Left on Dellwood St.
- 0.5 Right on 2nd Ave. NW.
- 0.8 Left on Cypress St.
- 1.1 Right on 6th Ave. NW.
- 1.3 Left on County Rd. 33 (N. Main St.).
- 4.7 Left on County 6.
- 7.7 Right on County 14.
- 10.6 Left on County 3.
- 12.6 Left on County 1.

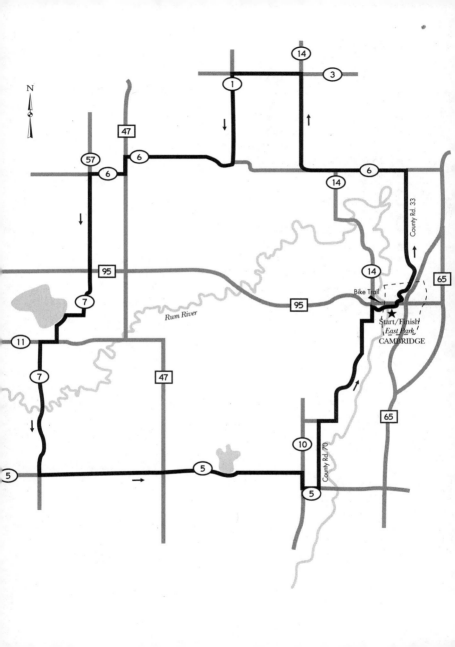

- 15.3 Right on County 6.
- 18.4 Left on Hwy. 47. **Caution: The road is narrow, and traffic may be heavy.**
- 18.9 Right on County 6.
- 19.9 Left on County 57.
- 22.9 Proceed straight across Hwy. 95 onto County 7.
- 25.6 Right on County 11.
- 26.1 Left on County 7.
- 30.2 Left on County 5.
- 33.7 Straight across Hwy. 47 onto County 5.
- 37.7 Right on County 10.
- 38.2 Left on County 5.
- 38.8 Left on County Rd. 70.
- 45.6 Right on the bike trail across from Cambridge Community College, through West Park and across the Rum River.
- 46.1 Arrive at parking lot.

Duluth North Shore Cruise

At the west end of Lake Superior lie the Twin Ports, Duluth and Superior, and one of the Midwest's most original bike trails. The Willard Munger State Trail is used as part of the annual Duluth North Shore Cycling Tour, held the first weekend of August. The loops shown here are two of three offered; the tour also includes a 100-mile route.

Western Lake Superior occupies a graben, a geologic feature created when a section of the earth's crust sinks between two fault lines. More than a billion years ago, lava welled up through fissures until it was 5 miles thick. The tremendous weight caused the earth's crust to subside. Tilted, jagged layers of lava give the area much of its character.

As you begin the gradual 400-foot ascent out of the lowland on the Willard Munger State Trail, you'll ride through a cut in the lava made when the railroad was pushed through. The prismatic rock fractures tell you the cut isn't a natural feature. The sunken basin of Lake Superior became an easy route for lobes of the continental glaciers that have invaded the area four times in the last million years. The ice sheets scraped and rounded the hardened lava, and in places you can see striations, rows of scratches on the rock face that indicate which direction the ice was moving.

Near Carlton the trail crosses the St. Louis River on an old stressed-iron bridge, a good spot to pause and look at the tilted layers of slate that seem to defy the erosive power of the fast-flowing water. A short distance farther you'll leave the trail and wind through the park on Highway 210. There will be several more good views of the river as you roll along. It's a great roll, too. You'll drop 400 feet in 8 miles with hardly a positive grade.

If you continue on into Duluth to complete the long route, you will gain all 400 feet back in a short 1.5 miles on Central Avenue and Highland Street. This will get you to Skyline Drive and a grand overview of the Twin Ports harbor. You'll see a great panorama of the harbor's industry and shipping.

You'll see Duluth's symbol, the Aerial Lift Bridge, spanning the channel that pierces the sandbar at the harbor's entrance. This is an international port, and each season oceangoing ships from Europe, Asia, South America, and Africa ply their way through the St. Lawrence Seaway and the Great Lakes to dock at the tall grain elevators and take on the harvest of America's heartland.

The Basics

Start: Park at the trailhead lot of the Willard Munger State Trail on 75th Ave. W. 1 block southeast of Hwy. 23 (Grand Ave.) in West Duluth.

Length: 31.6 or 46.1 miles.

Terrain: Flat, with a very long gradual climb on the Willard Munger State Trail.

Food: There are a great many options in Duluth. The Willard Munger Inn at the trailhead has a restaurant. A grocery and tavern are in Carlton.

For more information: Duluth North Shore Cycling Tour, Velo Duluth Cycle Club, 1205 93rd Ave. W. Duluth, MN 55808; Mark Lennon, (218) 626–3574. Duluth Convention and Visitors Bureau, Endion Station, 100 Lake Place Dr., Duluth, MN 55802; (800) 438–5884.

Bicycle service: Several locations in Duluth.

Miles & Directions

- 0.0 Ride southwest from the Willard Munger State Trail parking lot at 75th Ave. W.
- 14.5 Turn around at the village of Carlton, where you'll find a grocery store and a tavern.

- 15.7 Right on Hwy. 210. **Caution: The road is winding, and recreational vehicles may be encountered.**
- 23.8 Left on Hwy. 23/39. **Use caution and ride on the paved shoulder because significant traffic may be encountered.**
- 26.6 Continue straight on Hwy. 23 when Hwy. 39 turns right.

If you are riding the 31.6-mile route, turn right at mile 31.5 on 75th Ave. W. At mile 31.6 you'll arrive at the Willard Munger State Trail parking lot.

- 33.2 Left on Central Ave.
- 33.7 Left on Highland St.
- 34.7 Right on Skyline Dr.
- 36.8 Left on Haines Rd.
- 36.9 Right on Skyline Dr.
- 39.9 Bear right on 6th St. W.
- 40.0 Right on 11th Ave. W. **Caution: steep downhill.**
- 40.4 Right on 1st St. W.
- 42.1 Left on 30th Ave. W.
- 42.2 Right on W. Superior St., which becomes W. Michigan St.
- 42.9 Right on 40th Ave. W.
- 43.0 Left on W. Superior St., which becomes 1st St. W.
- 43.6 Straight onto Callalio Dr.
- 44.0 Straight onto Ramsey St.
- 44.2 Right on Central Ave.
- 44.4 Left on Grand Ave.
- 46.0 Left on 75th Ave. W.
- 46.1 Arrive at Willard Munger State Trail parking lot.

26

Headwaters Challenge

Northern Minnesota is the land of the mythical giant lumberjack Paul Bunyan. Legends tell of Paul clearing whole forests with a swing of his ax. The truth was that, to the lumber barons, every tree had a dollar sign on it, and they brought armies of men and animals to cut the trees and leave behind a landscape as desolate as the moon.

This tour of the Northwoods is part of the Headwaters Hundred, held annually on the last Saturday in September. Nearly 1,000 riders a year roll out of the old logging town of Park Rapids on 100-mile or -kilometer routes. On the way north on U.S. Highway 71, the route passes the Summerhill Farms restaurant, noted for its fresh lemonade and pies. Along the road you'll see larger second-growth trees mixed with stands of smaller aspen trees. Aspen is the popular species in logging these days; it regenerates in a mere twenty years and is used to make chipboard panels for building construction.

Entering Itasca State Park you'll be enthralled by the stately, old-growth forest, just as Jacob Brower was before he became the driving force behind creating Itasca State Park in 1891. The huge white and red pines inspire a reverence for nature that a managed, harvested forest never can.

Brower came to Lake Itasca to put to rest a controversy over the true source of the Mississippi River. In 1832 Indian agent Henry Rowe Schoolcraft had been guided by Ojibwa chief Ozawindib to the northern tip of Lake Itasca, where a small stream spilled out of the lake to begin its journey as the longest river in North America. Schoolcraft would go on to compile the Ojibwa legends he'd heard into a book that inspired the poet Longfellow to write "The Song of Hiawatha," but over the years his claim about the river's source was disputed.

Brower verified that Lake Itasca was the point of origin. While he was there, the beauty of the forest made him determined to save it from logging. He drafted a bill that passed the state legislature by one vote, and Itasca became Minnesota's first state park.

You can appreciate the majesty of the pines best by taking the paved bicycle trail that runs parallel to County 38 through a stand of 250-year-old red pines at Preacher's Grove. A spur path leads to the Mississippi Headwaters, and a short walk will take you to the actual point where the river emerges from the lake. If you like, you can wade across or step from stone to stone—it's only 30 feet across.

On Wilderness Drive you'll enter the Itasca Wilderness Sanctuary, a 2,000-acre area where no trees have been cut since 1939. Farther on you'll pass the Bison Kill Site—an archaeological excavation found that 8,000 years ago Paleo-Indians had tricked a herd of bison into a soft, swampy bog where they were easily killed. A few miles later you can take a short side trip to the Aiton Heights observation tower, where you can look out at forest and lake scenery as far as the eye can see, with no sign of manmade construction.

Douglas Lodge, located where Wilderness Drive rejoins County 1, features lodging and food, including a popular Sunday brunch and regular menu items like wild rice and walleyed pike. At the gift shop you can buy an award that commemorates your crossing of the Mississippi.

After retracing U.S. Highway 71, the route follows county roads through the scenic lake country north of Park Rapids. The striking aquamarine color of Blue Lake comes from an unusual algae in its water. At Emmaville you'll find the old-time Emmaville Cafe, where owner Cal Johnson is as much a part of the attraction as the menu.

The Basics

Start: Park at Heartland Park, 0.25 mile north of Hwy. 34 on Mill Rd. in Park Rapids.
Length: 60.3 or 81.2 miles.

Terrain: Flat to rolling.

Food: There are many restaurant and grocery opportunities in Park Rapids. On U.S. Hwy. 71, at the junction of County 40, is Summerhill Farms restaurant. In Itasca State Park, near the junction of County 48 and County 1, is a restaurant at Douglas Lodge. There is a soft drink machine at the headwaters of the Mississippi. At the junction of County 4 and County 24 is the Emmaville Cafe. There are five restaurants just south of the route in Dorset.

For more information: Headwaters 100, Park Rapids Chamber of Commerce, P.O. Box 249, Park Rapids, MN 56470; (800) 247–0054.

Bicycle service: In Park Rapids.

Miles & Directions

- 0.0 Proceed south on Mill Rd. from Heartland Park.
- 0.3 Right on Hwy. 34 (1st St.) to Park Rapids, where you'll find a number of restaurants and groceries.
- 0.6 Right on U.S. Hwy. 71 (N. Park Ave.). **Use caution and ride on the wide, paved shoulder because significant traffic may be encountered.**
- 20.9 Left on Hwy. 200.
- 21.3 Left on County 48 into the east entrance of Itasca State Park.
- 22.4 Right on County 1.
- 22.5 Right on the paved bicycle trail. **Caution: The path is twisty and traffic is two-way.**
- 24.5 Continue straight across County 38 on the bicycle trail.
- 27.3 Left on the bicycle trail spur to the Mississippi Headwaters.
- 27.4 Turn around and return to the main bicycle trail.
- 27.5 Left on the main bicycle trail.
- 27.6 Proceed straight into the parking lot; head for the lot entrance.
- 27.7 Left onto Wilderness Dr.
- 29.7 Left on Wilderness Dr. at the dead-end road to the boat landing.
- 37.9 Right on County 1.

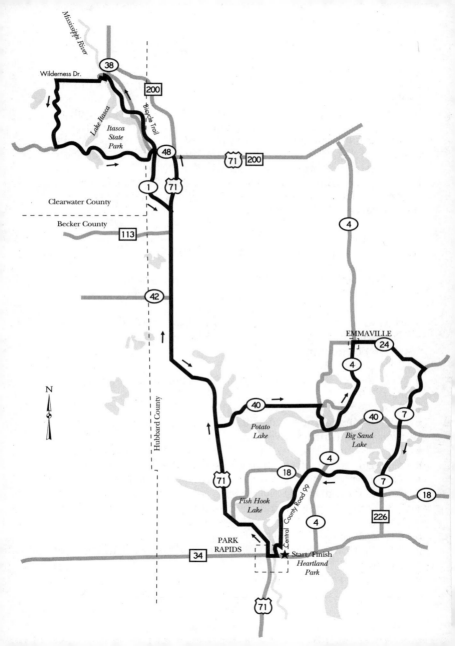

- 41.1 Right on U.S. Hwy. 71.
- 52.2 Left on County 40 to complete the long route.

If you are riding the shorter 60.3-mile route, continue straight on U.S. Hwy. 71 to Park Rapids. At mile 59.7 turn left on Hwy. 34. At mile 60.0 turn left on Mill Rd. At mile 60.3 you will arrive at Heartland Park.

- 58.8 Left on County 4.
- 63.3 Right on County 24.
- 67.0 Right on County 7.
- 73.1 Right on County 18.
- 77.0 Left on County Rd. 99, which becomes Central Ave.
- 80.7 Right on North St.
- 81.2 Arrive at Heartland Park.

Ohio

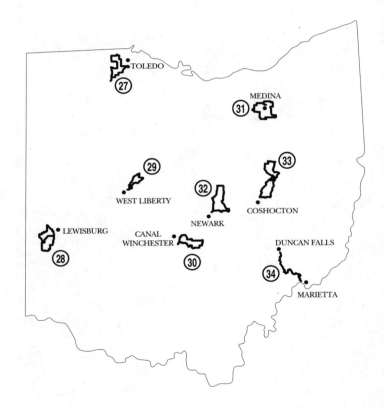

TOLEDO

㉗

MEDINA

㉛

㉝

㉙

WEST LIBERTY

㉜

COSHOCTON

LEWISBURG

CANAL
WINCHESTER

NEWARK

DUNCAN FALLS

㉘

㉚

㉞

MARIETTA

Ohio

27

Metroparks Cruise

In mid-July the Toledo Area Council of Hostelling International hosts its annual Metroparks Bicycle Tour. It includes 10-, 31-, and 100-mile loops in addition to the route depicted here. On this loop you visit four of Toledo's Metroparks with an added side trip to historic Fort Meigs.

The tour begins at Oak Openings Preserve Metropark, which provides 3,668 acres of habitat for many of Ohio's threatened and endangered species. More than 1,000 species of plants have been identified among the groves of white and black oak trees. Keep an eye open for sightings of bluebirds, indigo buntings, whippoorwills, white-tailed deer, mink, weasels, and fox.

Riding north of Oak Openings, you pass through countryside that is a mixture of farmland and creeping suburbia on your way to Secor Metropark. Secor is a contrast of old- and second-growth forest. Two magnificent white oak trees in front of the cemetery on Wolfinger Road predate European arrival.

Jogging south and east you come to the historic towns of Maumee and Perrysburg. The latter is the site of the restored stockade of Fort Meigs, the largest walled fortification in America. The sprawling system of earthen embankments topped with a spiked log palisade was built during the War of 1812 by William Henry Harrison.

Fort Meigs is not very formidable to look at, but in the spring of 1813 it withstood twelve days of British bombardment and the combined attack of the redcoats and their Indian allies. The English artillery included mortars capable of lobbing exploding shells into the fort, wreaking havoc upon the garrison. Harrison's clever system of zigzagging trenches within the fort neutralized their effectiveness, and the British were dealt their first significant defeat of the war.

Harrison's repulse caused the tribes to lose faith in the primacy of the British, and without large numbers of warrior allies, eventual American victory in the war was certain. The fort is open daily, and the museum and reenactments can be seen Wednesday through Sunday during the summer months.

Riding west from Maumee you'll pass the thin strip of Side Cut Metropark, overlooking the Maumee River and a section of the old Miami-Erie Canal. Deer are plentiful in the river bottom, and your chances of spotting them are good, especially late in the day.

You'll find Waterville still has much of the character of an old canal town. For a closer look at everyday life in that era, a stop at Providence Park is a must. The park features the restored Isaac Ludwig Mill, an operating water-powered 1847 mill, where grain is milled and lumber sawn. You can ride the dirt-surface Blue/Towpath Trail 0.5 mile west to the dock of the steamboat *Shawnee Princess* and 0.25 mile east to a restored section of the Miami-Erie Canal with an operating canal passenger boat.

The Basics

Start: Park at the All-Purpose Trailhead parking lot in Oak Openings Preserve Metropark, 1.5 miles east of Rte. 64.

Length: 69.0 miles.

Terrain: Flat.

Food: There is a concession stand in Oak Openings Preserve Metropark that is open on weekends. In Maumee and Perrysburg there are restaurants, groceries, and convenience stores. There are restaurants and an ice cream shop in Waterville. If needed, you can continue south from Providence Metropark across the Maumee River to the town of Grand Rapids, where you'll find restaurants and an ice cream shop.

For more information: Metroparks Bicycle Tour, Toledo Council AYH, P.O. Box 352736, Toledo, OH 43635-2736; (419) 841–4510. Greater Toledo Convention and Visitors Bureau, 401 Jefferson Ave., Toledo, OH 43604; (419) 321–6404 or (800) 243–4667.

Bicycle service: In Perrysburg.

Miles & Directions

- 0.0 Ride south out of the All-Purpose Trailhead parking lot.
- 0.1 Left on Oak Openings Pkwy.
- 1.4 Right on Rte. 295 (Berkley Southern Rd.).
- 1.6 Left on Obee Rd.
- 3.7 Left on Eber Rd.
- 7.9 Left on Garden Rd.
- 8.8 Left on Shaffer Rd.
- 11.8 Right on Lathrop Rd.
- 15.6 Right on Bancroft Rd.
- 19.0 Left on Tupelo Way, into Secor Metropark.
- 20.2 Right on Wolfinger Rd. in Secor Metropark.
- 21.6 Left on Bancroft Rd.
- 21.9 Right on Crissey Rd.
- 24.3 Left on Angola Rd.
- 25.6 Right on Albion Rd.
- 30.3 Left on Monclova Rd.
- 33.8 Straight across U.S. Hwy. 24 onto Wayne St.
- 34.9 Right on U.S. Hwy. 20 (Conant St.) in the town of Maumee, where you'll find groceries, restaurants, and convenience stores. **Use caution crossing the Maumee River bridge on U.S. Hwy. 20. because significant traffic may be encountered. A sidewalk on the bridge can be ridden to avoid traffic.**
- 35.7 Bear right on Rte. 25 (W. Boundary St.) in Perrysburg, where you'll find groceries, restaurants, and convenience stores.
- 36.0 Right on Rte. 65.
- 36.6 Turn around at entrance to Fort Meigs State Memorial.
- 37.2 Left on Rte. 25 (W. Boundary St.).
- 37.5 Left on U.S. Hwy. 20.
- 38.3 Left in Maumee onto Broadway, which becomes River Rd.
- 43.8 Right on Waterville Rd. in the town of Waterville, where you'll find restaurants and an ice cream shop.
- 46.5 Left on Howard Rd.
- 48.1 Right on Neowash Rd.
- 50.3 Left on Heller Rd.
- 51.9 Right on Box Rd.

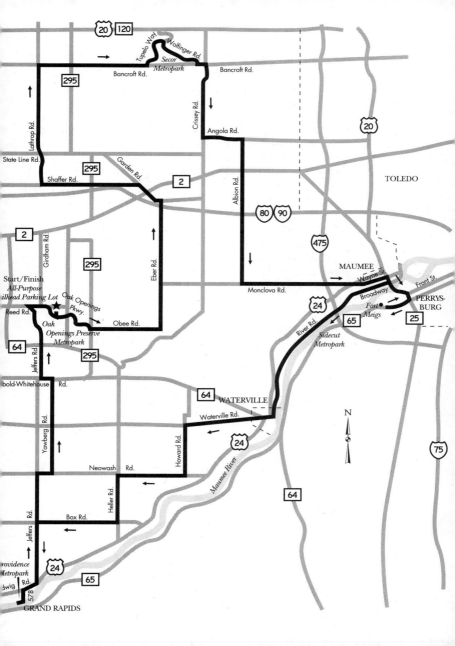

- 54.4 Left on Jeffers Rd.
- 56.4 Right on Ludwig Rd. at the intersection with U.S. Hwy. 24.
- 56.8 Left on Rte. 578.
- 57.1 Straight across U.S. Hwy. 24 on Rte. 578, and make an immediate right into Providence Metropark, Isaac Ludwig Mill parking lot. **Use caution at this busy intersection.**
- 57.2 Turn around at Isaac Ludwig Mill.
- 57.3 Left on Rte. 578, and straight across U.S. Hwy. 24.
- 57.6 Right on Ludwig Rd.
- 58.0 Left on Jeffers Rd.
- 61.5 Right on Neowash Rd.
- 62.0 Left on Yawberg Rd.
- 65.1 Left on Archbold-Whitehouse Rd.
- 65.5 Right on Jeffers Rd.
- 67.9 Right on Reed Rd.
- 68.3 Straight onto Oak Openings Pkwy. at intersection with Girdham Rd.
- 68.9 Left into All-Purpose Trailhead parking lot.
- 69.0 Arrive at parking lot.

28

Dog Days of Summer Cruise

On the first Saturday of August, 500 riders fill up the annual Dog Days of Summer ride. They know they're not in for a crack-of-dawn experience. The 8:30 A.M. start time, with a continental breakfast and an invitation to stash as many goodies as you can carry, sets the tone for a tour that's kind to volunteers and riders alike.

Tour organizer Mark Garlikov claims that it's been banned by three major diet programs, and he's dubbed the event a "Tri-Eat-A-Thon," even copyrighting the name. The three aspects are biking, eating, and swimming. There are as many as five swimming stops on the 72-mile route that the tour offers, in addition to the 48.2- and 34.7-mile loops shown here. A 12-mile loop is also offered. Swimming fees are included in the entry, as are breakfast, a lunch blow-out, a coupon for the Dairy Queen, and watermelon at the finish.

The tour starts at the community park in the quaint little town of Lewisburg, where you can still find 25-cent pop machines. The route rolls south through scenic farmland where dairy cows and hogs are raised. Even if you're riding the tour by yourself, there's no reason for not stopping at the swimming pool on your way out of West Alexandria.

As you near the town of Eaton, you'll pass Fort St. Clair State Park, which marks the site of Mad Anthony Wayne's victory over the French in the French and Indian War. A festival of period exhibits and reenactments is held each year on the last weekend of September. Just outside Eaton is another community swimming pool.

Riding north on your way back to Lewisburg, you'll visit two covered bridges. These are great photo opportunities as you ride your bike across them. The Christman Bridge, built in 1895, is located just off the route, on Eaton–New Hope Road where Gettysburg Road splits off. The 1894 Geeting Bridge is on Price Road, and you have to ride through it; it's part of the route.

When you finish your ride, you may want to end it in the Tri-Eat-A-Thon tradition. The place to do so is at the Midway Restaurant, 0.25 mile west of Route 503 on U.S. Highway 40. It's famous for pork tenderloin steak, onion rings, and homemade pies.

The Basics

Start: Lewisburg Community Park on E. Dayton St., 0.25 mile east of Rte. 503.

Length: 34.7 or 48.2 miles.

Terrain: Flat to rolling.

Food: There are restaurants, a grocery, and an ice cream shop in Lewisburg. In West Alexandria you'll find restaurants and groceries. There are restaurants and a grocery in Eaton. At the intersection of U.S. Hwy. 127 and Price Rd., there is a Dairy Queen.

For more information: Dog Days of Summer, Dog Days Bicycle Touring Society, 308 Talbott Tower, Dayton, OH 45402; (937) 222–1710; Web site: www.dogdays.org. Eaton–Preble County Chamber of Commerce, 204 N. Barron St., Eaton, OH 45320; (513) 456–4949.

Miles & Directions

- 0.0 Ride south out of the Lewisburg Community Park parking lot and turn left on Lewisburg-Salem Rd.
- 0.4 Bear right on Lewisburg-Ozias Rd. at the intersection with Salem Rd.
- 1.1 Straight onto Lewisburg-Ozias Rd. at the intersection where Lewisburg Rd. goes to the left.
- 1.9 Right on New Market–Banta Rd.

If you are riding the 34.7-mile route, turn right at mile 3.3 on Brennersville-Pyrmont Rd. At mile 6.2 proceed straight onto Eaton-Lewisburg Rd. At mile 6.6 bear left onto Eaton-Lewisburg Rd. Turn left at mile 9.7 on T–424 (Cottingham Rd.), which becomes East Ave. At mile 11.5 turn right on U.S. Hwy. 35 (Main St.) in the town of Eaton. At mile 12.4 turn right on Park Ave. From here pick up the directions below at mile 25.9.

- 7.7 Right on U.S. Hwy. 35 in the town of West Alexandria, where you'll find restaurants and groceries.
- 8.0 Left on Rte. 503. You'll find the West Alexandria swimming pool to the left, on Smith St.
- 9.6 Right on Fisher-Twin Rd.
- 11.2 Left on Twin Rd.
- 14.0 Right on Carlton Rd.
- 14.7 Right on Rte. 122.
- 15.0 Left on Quaker-Trace Rd.
- 16.0 Right on Central Rd.
- 18.2 Left on 7 Mile Rd.
- 20.4 Right on Camden Rd.
- 23.0 Left on Consolidated Rd.; then make an immediate right on Camden Rd.
- 23.7 Left on Camden Rd. at the intersection of Kincaid Rd.
- 25.2 Right on Rte. 122 (swimming pool at top of hill).
- 25.9 Left on Park Ave. in the town of Eaton, where you'll find restaurants and a grocery. Park Ave. becomes Eaton–New Hope Rd.
- 28.2 Bear right on Gettysburg Rd. where Eaton–New Hope Rd. veers left.
- 30.2 Right on Spacht Rd.
- 32.0 Right on Winnerline Rd.
- 32.8 Left on Rte. 726.
- 33.0 Right on Winnerline Rd.
- 33.8 Left on Central Rd.
- 34.6 Right on Orphens Rd.
- 35.8 Left on U.S. Hwy. 127. **Caution: Significant traffic may be encountered.**
- 36.5 Right on Price Rd., where you'll find a Dairy Queen.
- 38.9 Left on Yohe Rd.
- 42.6 Right on Euphemia-Castine Rd.
- 46.6 Right on Rte. 503.
- 47.7 Left on E. Dayton St. in the town of Lewisburg, where you'll find restaurants, an ice cream shop, and a grocery.
- 48.2 Left into Lewisburg Community Park; arrive at parking lot.

29

Crossroads Ramble

The roads in west-central Ohio go every which way. Farther west the layout becomes geometric, with roads running north-south and east-west and having ninety-degree corners. It seems that around West Liberty order wasn't a high priority. Perhaps the early settlers followed old Indian trails or just wanted to take the scenic route. All this works wonders for bicyclists.

There's something about the road that twists and turns that spells adventure and surprise. It may be an avenue of maples, a ridgetop view, or a babbling stream. The Crossroads Bike Tour, held annually on the first Saturday of August, weaves its routes through this pretty, hilly countryside. In addition to this loop, the tour offers 15- and 62-mile routes.

Ohio isn't thought of much in the history of the Civil War. Many Ohio soldiers served the Union, but no major battles were fought here. The history of our nation might have been different, though, were it not for the actions of Ohio's conscientious citizens. In the years before the Civil War, Ohio became a hotbed of abolitionist sentiment. It was not an easy struggle. In the 1830s, when a handful of students, teachers, and clergy began to rail against the immorality of slavery and the belief that blacks were innately inferior, they were often in fear of their lives.

As time passed more people became persuaded by the justness of their cause. Ohio became a key area for what was known as the Underground Railroad, a system of sympathetic citizens who were willing to shelter and hide fugitive slaves as they made their way from bondage south of the Ohio River to freedom in Canada. It was a risky business. It was illegal to help runaway slaves, and many people did not believe in the cause. Federal law allowed slave catchers to roam northern states at will. Often they tried to capture free blacks and take them south.

The Pioneer House, just off the route on T–47 east of West Liberty, was a station on the Underground Railroad. The eleven-room log house was the home of Judge Benjamin Piatt and his wife, Elizabeth. Only Elizabeth was an abolitionist, though. She would hang a flag on the hitching post in front of the house if the judge wasn't home—a signal that it was safe to stop.

The Underground Railroad movement could help only a tiny fraction of people, but it polarized the nation. When Abraham Lincoln was elected, southerners rebelled against having an abolitionist president. Two of the Piatts' sons served with distinction as officers in the Civil War. When the war was over, they abandoned their simple log cabin roots and built the Piatt Castles: huge, limestone tributes to Victorian excess that can be seen from the route. These mansions can be toured daily during the riding season. The Pioneer House is now an antiques shop and is open daily.

The Basics

Start: Park at Village Park, just east of the Mad River off of Rte. 245 (Baird Street) in West Liberty.
Length: 31.7 miles.
Terrain: Rolling to hilly.
Food: There are several restaurants, a grocery, and an ice cream parlor in West Liberty. Zanesfield and East Liberty have country grocery stores.
For more information: Crossroads Bike Tour, Pedal Power Bicycle Shop, 114 S. Detroit St., West Liberty, OH 43357; (937) 465–6525. Greater Logan County Convention & Tourism Bureau, 100 S. Main St., Bellefontaine, OH 43311; (937) 599–5121 or (800) LOGANCO.
Bicycle service: In West Liberty.

Miles & Directions

- 0.0 Ride south from the parking lot out of Village Park.
- 0.1 Left on Rte. 245 (Baird St.).

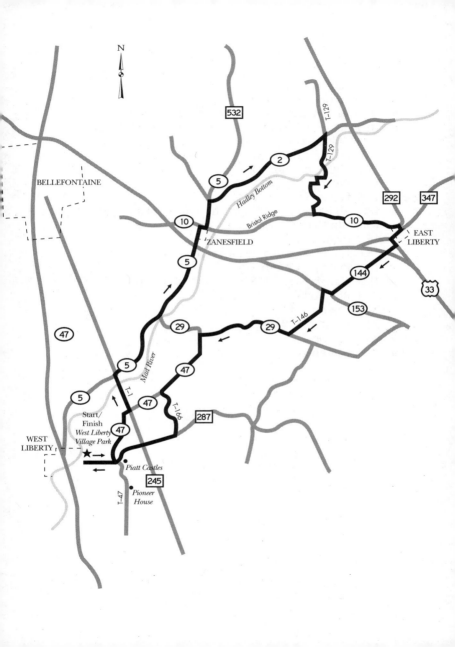

- 1.0 Left on County 47.
- 2.6 Left on T–1.
- 3.7 Right on County 5.
- 8.0 Straight across U.S. Hwy. 33 onto County 5.
- 8.5 Right on County 10/5 in the village of Zanesfield, where you'll find a country grocery store.
- 8.6 Left on County 5.
- 9.6 Right on County 2.
- 13.3 Right on T–129.
- 15.9 Left on County 10.
- 18.1 Right on Rte. 292 in the village of East Liberty, where you'll find a country grocery store.
- 18.3 Right on Rte. 347.
- 18.6 Left on an unnamed town road.
- 18.8 Right on County 144.
- 19.3 Straight across U.S. Hwy. 33 onto County 144.
- 21.1 Right on County 153.
- 21.3 Left on T–146.
- 23.1 Right on County 29.
- 25.7 Left on County 47.
- 27.5 Left on T–166.
- 29.0 Right on Rte. 287.
- 30.0 Straight onto Rte. 245.
- 31.6 Right into Village Park.
- 31.7 Arrive at Village Park parking lot.

30

Covered Bridge Ramble

In the United States, Ohio is second only to Pennsylvania in the number of covered bridges still standing. More than 130 of these unique structures can be found spanning streams on narrow country roads or relocated in town parks in the southern half of the state. For more than a dozen years, the Columbus Council of American Youth Hostels has been staging a tour that takes in many of these bridges that seem to symbolize a less complicated, more peaceful time long past. This route is part of the annual Covered Bridge Century that takes place on the second weekend of September. Other loops are 60 and 100 miles in length.

Fairfield County has one of the highest concentrations of covered bridges in Ohio. While they seem nostalgic reminders of our bucolic roots, in their heyday, in the midnineteenth century, they were considered high-tech. The invention of the truss system of interlocking triangles made possible strong, inexpensive wooden spans of great length. The barnlike wooden covers were added to protect the trusses from the weather. A variety of truss designs were used, but integrity and craftsmanship were the marks that have allowed them to endure into our era.

The bridges brought access and mobility to rural America, where previously a trip to town often included fording dangerous streams. Culturally, the bridges were more than that. They were symbolic of the march of civilization, shelter in a rainstorm, and shade on a sunny day. The play of light and shadow through the boards and trusses made them special places. The moments of wonder and privacy of a crossing made them favorite places for young couples to steal a kiss on a buggy ride. Wooden bridges remained popular even after the introduction of iron-and-steel structures. Covered bridges were cheaper to build and, perhaps, too dear to give up.

The little town of Canal Winchester is an interesting collection of historic buildings and small shops and museums. The Ohio-Erie Canal and, later, the railroad and interurban railway brought a fine measure of comfort and prosperity to the tree-lined streets. The Shades Restaurant, on High Street, is popular for its family-style meals and is a good place to stop before or after the ride. Your tour begins with a short out-and-back run to an old road south of town to see the Dietz-Burgstresser Bridge, the last covered bridge in Franklin County still open to traffic. As you pass through, pause a moment in the soft light to listen to the sounds of Walnut Creek.

Back in Canal Winchester you'll head east along the route of the old Ohio Canal to the crossroads village of Lockville, where the Hartman Bridge sits in the town park along with a lock from the canal. The easy ride past fields of corn and soybeans will lead you to two more covered bridges. Along Basil-Western Road you'll see the Shryer Bridge relocated in a farmyard, and on the edge of Pickerington the Zeller-Smith Bridge is located in a small park. With a little luck you'll come away from this ride with covered bridge memories of your own.

The Basics

Start: Park on the street at the restored Canal Winchester Railroad Depot and begin riding from the intersection of Railroad St. and High St.

Length: 33.7 miles.

Terrain: Flat to gently rolling.

Food: There are a grocery and several restaurants in Canal Winchester. In Carroll you'll find a general store, a pizza shop, and taverns. In Baltimore there are a grocery store and a cafe.

For more information: Covered Bridge Century, c/o Brian Sittler, 48 W. Mound St., Canal Winchester, OH 43110; (614) 833–0357. Canal Winchester Area Chamber of Commerce, P.O. Box 74, Canal Winchester, OH 43110; (614) 837–1556, FAX (614) 837–5901.

Miles & Directions

- 0.0 Ride south on High St. from the Canal Winchester Depot.

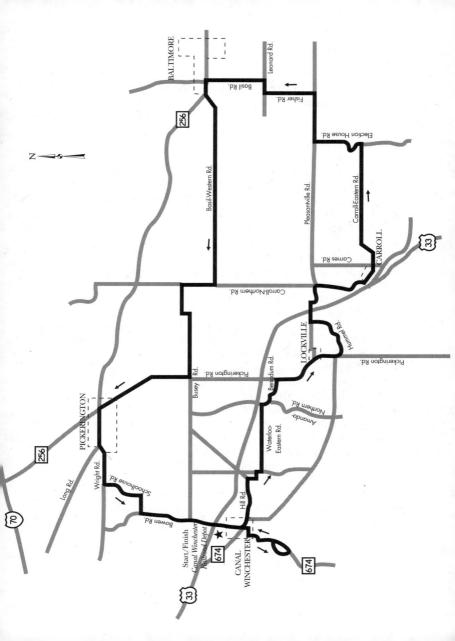

- 0.3 Right on Columbus St.
- 0.5 Left on County 674 (Washington St.).
- 1.1 Right on a narrow road just before County 674 crosses Walnut Creek; follow the sign to the Dietz-Burgstresser Bridge.
- 1.5 Left on County 674.
- 2.4 Right on Columbus St.
- 2.6 Left on High St.
- 2.7 Right on Waterloo St., which becomes Hill Rd.
- 3.8 Right on Waterloo Rd.
- 4.0 Right on Diley Rd. in the village of Waterloo.
- 4.1 Straight onto Waterloo-Eastern Rd.
- 5.7 Right on Amanda-Northern Rd.
- 6.0 Left on Benadum Rd.
- 6.5 Right on Pickerington Rd.
- 7.5 Bear right in the village of Lockville.
- 8.2 Left on Hummel Rd.
- 9.5 Right on Pleasantville Rd.
- 10.3 Right on Carroll-Northern Rd.
- 11.5 Bear left on Carroll-Eastern Rd. in the village of Carroll, where you'll find a general store, a pizza shop, and taverns.
- 14.6 Left on Election House Rd.
- 15.7 Right on Pleasantville Rd.
- 16.7 Left on Fisher Rd.
- 17.7 Right on Leonard Rd.
- 17.8 Left on Basil Rd.
- 19.0 Left on Rte. 256 in the village of Baltimore, where you'll find a grocery store and a cafe.
- 19.2 Bear left onto Basil-Western Rd.
- 23.5 Right on Carroll-Northern Rd.
- 24.2 Left on Busey Rd.
- 26.5 Right on Pickerington Rd.
- 28.6 Left Rte. 256 (Main St.) in the village of Pickerington.
- 28.9 Straight on Wright Rd.
- 30.3 Left on Schoolhouse Rd.
- 31.5 Left on Bowen Rd.
- 33.7 Arrive at Canal Winchester Depot.

31

Ice Cream Cruise

Everyone knows that ice cream is the rocket fuel of bicycling. When the Medina County Bicycle Club was looking to organize a tour in its area, the assets were obvious. You could get ice cream almost anywhere. A sponsorship from local Stop and Go stores, convenience purveyors of frozen delights, sealed the deal. Held on the last Saturday in July, the tour visits seven ice cream stops on the 57-mile route and four on the 40. And ice cream is served at the start and the finish. For short hitters the tour also offers a 15-mile loop with only two ice cream opportunities.

If you're riding the route on your own, the tour begins in downtown Medina at the picturesque Public Square, with its Victorian gazebo. Perhaps you feel you're missing out on the ice cream–propelled start by not riding the organized tour? Fear not—there are several opportunities to load up on the way out of town. A few blocks west of the public square, you'll pass Root's West Liberty Commons, a gift shop, deli, and ice cream parlor in a restored landmark building. On the outskirts of town, you'll see the tour's first official ice cream stop at an ever-reliable Stop and Go store.

Just to make you feel that you've earned your ice cream reward, the route dishes out its hilliest stretch early, on Fenn Road. Filled with a sense of physical accomplishment, you'll be primed for a visit to the ice cream shop at the village of River Styx. You won't have to wait long for the next opportunity. A few miles farther, at Wadsworth, you can choose between a Stop and Go and an ice cream shop.

Along Greenwich Road are several interesting sights. The Weltzen Skypark is a unique airport wherein homes are built along the runway and residents park planes in their garages. You'll also pass one of the area's buffalo farms, with a good chance of catching sight of a herd of these shaggy beasts. At the junction with Route 3, there's an ice cream restaurant. If you decide to take the short route back, your ice cream options will be at the Stop and Go's near Chippewa Lake and on the outskirts of Medina.

On the long route your next stop is the Dairy Queen in the village of Seville, where you'll also have a photo opportunity in front of the town barbershop. You guessed it—it's called the "Barber of Seville." At the junction of Westfield and Lafayette, there is a deli that serves ice cream. You'd best save some room for the last stop, in Chatham: The Goose & Gander Restaurant is part of Packard's General Store, and you can enjoy your ice cream on the porch of this rustic enterprise. Remember, ice cream doesn't travel well, but if you haven't packed in enough calories to make it back to Medina, you haven't really tried.

The Basics

Start: Park on the street at the Medina Public Square, and start at the corner of West Liberty St. and N. Court St.

Length: 40.2 or 57.5 miles.

Terrain: Flat, hilly, and rolling.

Food: There are groceries, numerous restaurants, and several ice cream shops and convenience stores in Medina. At Windfall there are restaurants and convenience stores. There is an ice cream shop in River Styx. At Wadsworth there are a convenience store and an ice cream shop. A combination ice cream shop and restaurant is located at the junction of Greenwich Rd. and Rte. 3. There is a Dairy Queen in Seville. At the junction of Greenwich Rd. and Lafayette Rd., there is a deli/ice cream shop. At Chatham you'll find a restaurant, ice cream shop, and general store. On the short route there is a convenience store/ice cream shop near Chippewa Lake.

For more information: David Schultz, Medina County Bicycle Club, 610 Berkshire Dr., Medina, OH 44256; (330) 725–0293. Medina County Convention & Visitors Bureau, 124 W. Lafayette Rd., Suite 100, Medina, OH 44256; (330) 722–5502 or (800) 860–2943.

Bicycle service: In Medina and Wadsworth.

Miles & Directions

- 0.0 Ride west on West Liberty St. from the intersection of N. Court St.
- 1.6 Right on Abbeyville Rd.
- 3.1 Right on Fenn Rd. **Caution: Ride on the paved shoulder because significant traffic may be encountered.**
- 3.8 Left on Marks Rd.
- 3.9 Right on Fenn Rd.
- 4.8 Straight across U.S. Hwy. 42 onto Fenn Rd.
- 7.2 Right on Rte. 3. **Caution: Ride on the paved shoulder because significant traffic may be encountered.**
- 7.6 Straight onto T–268 when Rte. 3 veers to the right.
- 7.7 Left on Cook Rd.
- 8.4 Right on Hood Rd.
- 9.5 Right on T–131.
- 10.1 Left on Granger Rd.
- 10.3 Right on Windfall Rd.
- 11.7 Straight across Rte. 18 onto Windfall Rd. at the Windfall truck stop, where you'll find restaurants and convenience stores.
- 12.7 Right on Plank Rd.
- 14.2 Left on River Styx Rd.
- 17.6 Left on Rte. 57.
- 18.6 Straight onto River Styx Rd. in the village of River Styx, where you'll find an ice cream shop.
- 19.4 Left on Blake Rd.
- 22.0 Right on Leatherman Rd.
- 23.4 Right on Greenwich Rd. on the outskirts of the town of Wadsworth, where you'll find a convenience store and an ice cream shop.
- 29.4 Left on Rte. 3. You'll find a combination ice cream shop and restaurant at this corner.

If you are riding the 40.2-mile route, continue straight on Greenwich Rd. and at mile 29.9 turn right on Ryan Rd. At mile 31.6 turn left on Kennard Rd. At mile 32.5 turn right on Lake Rd., along which you'll find a

convenience store/ice cream shop. At mile 35.8 turn right on Rte. 162. Turn left on Rte. 3 at mile 37.5. **Use caution and ride on the paved shoulder because significant traffic may be encountered.** *Arrive at the Medina Public Square at mile 40.2.*

- 30.4 Right on Rte 3. in the village of Seville, where you'll find a Dairy Queen.
- 30.6 Right on Seville Rd. when Rte. 3 veers to the left.
- 34.0 Right on Leroy Rd.
- 35.0 Left on Greenwich Rd.
- 35.5 Right on Lafayette Rd. You'll find a deli/ice cream shop at this intersection.
- 38.7 Left on Chippewa Rd.
- 39.7 Straight across U.S. Hwy. 42 onto Chippewa Rd.
- 42.2 Right on Vandemark Rd.
- 43.2 Left on Coon Club Rd.
- 44.4 Right on Rte. 83.
- 45.0 Right on Rte. 162 in the village of Chatham, where you'll find a restaurant, ice cream shop, and general store.
- 46.1 Left on Vandemark Rd.
- 48.6 Right on Smith Rd.
- 50.1 Left on Erhart Rd.
- 51.4 Right on Stone Rd.
- 55.0 Right on Rte. 57 (Norwalk Rd.), which becomes W. Liberty St. in Medina.
- 57.5 Arrive at Medina Public Square at N. Court St.

Land of Legend Challenge

"Land of Legend" is a fitting name for a bike tour starting in Newark. Lost in the mists of time are the voices and traditions of the Hopewell people who once lived here. Newark was the center of their influential culture, which thrived between 1000 B.C. and A.D. 300. They managed a vast trade network that stretched from Florida to Lake Superior. Their stunning, realistic art was very different from that of later cultures. Early scientists concocted bogus theories attributing the objects to a vanished race. In Newark, where they mined precious flint, the Hopewell people built fantastic, geometric earthen mounds.

At the Mound Builders State Memorial, where the ride begins, the earthwork is 14 feet high and 1,200 feet in diameter. You can view the work of the Hopewell and other cultures at the Ohio Indian Art Museum in Newark. The city is also the site of the National Heisey Glass Museum, home of the country's largest collection of glass figurines, which were produced in Newark from 1895 to 1957.

The ride has a history of its own, too. For the past twenty-two years, the Licking County Bicycle Club has organized the Land of Legend Tour on the second Saturday in June. The tour also includes a 100- and a 30-mile route in addition to this 60-mile loop.

East of Newark you'll ride across rolling terrain and soon arrive at one of the state's prettiest and historically most interesting bike trails. The Black Hand Gorge Bike Trail is a nature preserve. Its deep gorge, where the Licking River flows through black-hand sandstone, was created by glacial outwash. Unique flora, which is native much farther north, thrives in the gorge, protected by its shelter. The trail rises at times 30 to 40 feet above the river. You'll see remnants of the Ohio Canal that once crossed the state, including a preserved lock. An abandoned railroad tunnel was used for an electric trolley line that ran from Zanesville to Columbus.

North of the town of Hanover, you'll roll through the gentle terrain along a stream named Rocky Fork. As you turn onto Rain Rock Road, the route is hillier and the wooded scenery is punctuated by sandstone outcroppings. When you cross Route 586, you're at Henpeck Corners. You won't find anything there anymore; I just liked the name.

Farther on, the route rolls over moderately hilly farmland, with crops of corn, soybeans, and wheat, as well as the occasional cattle and horse farm. You'll also cruise through the small rural villages of Bladensburg, Martinsburg, and St. Louisville before returning to Newark.

The Basics

Start: Park at Mound Builders State Memorial, just off of Rte. 79 on the southside of the city of Newark. The park entrance is at 21st St., which is the city's main north-south street, and Cooper Ave.
Length: 59.9 miles.
Terrain: Rolling to moderately hilly.
Food: There are many restaurants and groceries in Newark. In Hanover there are a restaurant and a grocery just off-route. There's a country store in the crossroads village of Hickman. Bladensburg has a restaurant. In the village of Martinsburg, you'll find a Dairy Queen and a grocery. The village of St. Louisville is even more well appointed, with restaurants, an ice cream stand, and a grocery.
For more information: Licking County Bicycle Club, 432 Dorrence Rd. NE, Granville, OH 43023; (614) 587–4575. Newark Chamber of Commerce, 50 W. Locust St., Newark, OH 43055; (614) 345–9757.
Bicycle service: One shop with two locations in Newark.

Miles & Directions

■   0.0 Turn right, which is east, on Cooper Ave. at the entrance to Mound Builders State Memorial.

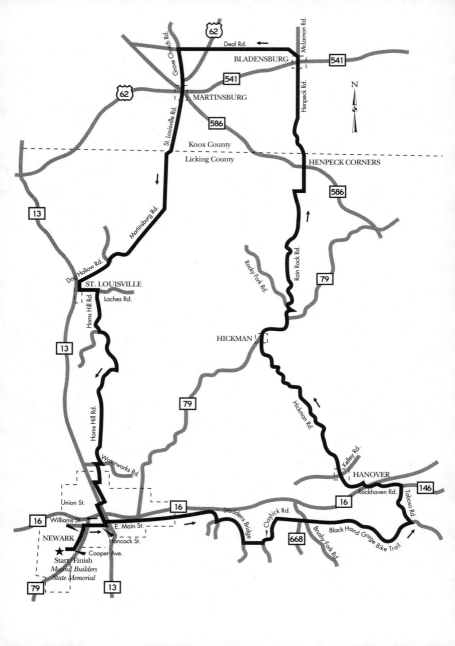

- 0.3 Left on Williams St.
- 0.4 Right on Hancock St.
- 0.5 Left on Union St.
- 1.2 Right on W. Main St., which becomes E. Main St. after circuiting Courthouse Square.
- 5.5 Right on Staddens Bridge Rd.
- 7.7 Left on Claylick Rd. **Use caution on the steep downhill and curve as you approach the intersection of Brushy Fork Rd.**
- 9.6 Proceed straight onto Brushy Fork Rd. The entrance to the Black Hand Gorge Bike Trail is not well marked. Look for large, green oil storage tanks and a parking lot entrance on the left 0.1 mile after you cross Rte. 668. You'll find the entrance to the bike path in the parking lot.
- 9.7 Left onto Black Hand Gorge Bike Trail.
- 13.9 Exit the bike trail into the parking lot, and turn left on Toboso Rd.
- 15.4 Left on Rockhaven Rd.
- 17.1 Right on 7 Hills Rd.; cross over the freeway.
- 17.2 Left on Marne Rd. **Use caution just before the village of Hanover at a railroad underpass with a blind curve.**
- 17.9 Right on Main St. into the village of Hanover, where you'll find a restaurant. There is also a grocery just off-route.
- 18.4 Proceed straight onto Hickman Rd. at the four-way stop.
- 24.4 Right on Rte. 79 (Fallsburg Rd.) at the crossroads village of Hickman, where you'll find a country store. **Use caution on this section because it is a busy, hilly, curvy road.**
- 25.9 Left on Rocky Fork Rd.
- 26.1 Right on Rain Rock Rd. **Use caution on the long downhill as you approach Rte. 586.**
- 31.3 Straight across Rte. 586 onto Rain Rock Rd.
- 31.6 At the Knox County Line, Rain Rock Rd. becomes Henpeck Rd.
- 34.6 Straight on McLarnan Rd. at Rte. 541 in the village of Bladensburg, where you'll find a restaurant.
- 34.8 Left on Hopewell Rd., which becomes Deal Rd.
- 38.7 Left on Grove Church Rd.

- 39.9 Right on U.S. Hwy. 62 (Millersburg Rd.).
- 40.3 At Rte. 541 go straight across onto St. Louisville Rd. in the village of Martinsburg, where you'll find a Dairy Queen and a grocery.
- 42.3 Proceed straight on St. Louisville Rd., which becomes Martinsburg Rd. at the Licking County line.
- 45.8 Straight onto Dog Hollow Rd.
- 48.3 Left on Sugar St. into the village of St. Louisville, where you'll find restaurants, an ice cream stand, and a grocery.
- 48.6 Left on Loches Rd.
- 49.2 Right on Horns Hill Rd.
- 55.4 Right on Waterworks Rd.
- 55.5 Left on Hollander St.
- 56.4 Right on Stevens St.
- 56.5 Left on Hudson St.
- 57.3 Right on St. Clair St.
- 57.4 At Rte. 13 go straight across onto Hoover St.
- 57.8 Left on 11th St.
- 57.9 Left on Granville St., then make an immediate right on 11th St.
- 58.5 Right on E. Main St.
- 59.0 Left on Williams St.
- 59.6 Right on Cooper Ave.
- 59.9 Arrive at Mound Builders State Memorial.

33

Roscoe Classic

In the early nineteenth century, Ohio was a complex of canals. They were the vogue in transportation before being eclipsed by the railroads. Canals linked the frontier with stately, mule-drawn boats that floated along at perfect speeds for enjoying the scenery. For twenty years, on the third weekend of August, the Akron Bicycle Club has promoted bicycle speed as the best way to see this historic area. The club's two-day tour, called the Roscoe Ramble, features an overnight in Coshocton, and the ride quickly fills its 150-person limit. A big attraction is the visit to Roscoe Village, the finest example of a restored canal port in the state. The ride dates coordinate with the town's Canal Days Festival. This one-day loop is based on the club's route.

With the arrival of the first canal boat in 1830, Roscoe began to prosper on the trade that flowed between the Ohio River and Lake Erie. The community became a showcase of hopeful brick stores and homes built in simple Federal and Greek Revival styles. Canal traffic began to slow with the coming of the railroad in 1850, and when the Flood of 1913 closed the canal for good, Roscoe had slid into neglect and disrepair. In 1960 a mural of the village's canal heyday was created for the Coshocton National Bank. The 24-foot-long painting inspired many local people to save Roscoe's decaying buildings. Today the town's authentic "canal days" atmosphere makes it one of the state's top tourist attractions.

You'll appreciate the easy roll at the start of this tour as you parallel the old canal route in the broad valley of the Tuscarawas River. People compare the scenery to finer parts of New England. The wooded hillsides lining the valley are a hint of things to come.

Turning north at West Lafayette, you'll begin winding through narrower and narrower valleys as the road traces the White Creek and Eyes Creek before climbing to the village of Baltic. By then you'll have gradually gained about 300 feet of elevation, but there's more to come. If this first climb is too much for you, there's the option of heading west to New Bedford and bypassing the hill country.

Over an 11-mile stretch before Winesburg are five steep, relentless climbs of 300 to 500 feet. This is Amish country. Midway you'll find the village of Walnut Creek and the Dutch Harvest Restaurant, which specializes in Amish food. Don't overeat though—there are three more climbs to Winesburg, and the last one is a whopping 550-footer with a long one-in-eight stretch. As you ride, enjoy the view, but keep a lookout for narrow buggy wheel ruts in the pavement that have been known to cause a spill.

The Amish religion proscribes the use of modern conveniences, and you may see more horse-drawn buggies than cars parked on the town streets in this area. Scenes of Amish life fit well in a bike tour based out of Coshocton, but you may wonder if these simple folk don't feel as if they're living their lives in a fishbowl. Roscoe Ramble tour organizer Bill Kelleher tells of struggling up a long hill in the middle of the day and finding a group of teenage Amish boys leaning against their buggies at the top. "How come you aren't working?" he asked. "We'd rather watch you work," one replied. So who's in the fishbowl?

Beyond Winesburg the hills continue, but 200-foot climbs prevail. South of New Bedford you'll drop more than 400 feet as you follow Mill Creek. At Roscoe Village you can reward yourself with dinner at the Roscoe Village Inn or the Warehouse Restaurant. Bicyclists rave about both—all in the cause of nutrition, of course.

The Basics

Start: Park in the free public parking lot on 5th St., between Chestnut St. and Main St. in Coshocton.
Length: 41.3 or 79.0 miles.
Terrain: Flat to very hilly.
Food: There are numerous options in Coshocton. In West Lafayette

there are restaurants, a grocery, and convenience stores. In Baltic you'll find a convenience store. There are several restaurants in Walnut Creek. In Winesburg you'll find restaurants and convenience stores. In Mt. Hope there is a grocery. At the junction of Boyd Rd. and U.S. Hwy. 62/Rte. 39, there is a restaurant. In the village of Charm, you'll find a restaurant. There are convenience stores in Farmerstown and New Bedford. In Roscoe Village there are several restaurants and an ice cream shop.

For more information: Roscoe Ramble, Akron Bicycle Club, P.O. Box 2268, Stow, OH 44224; (330) 922–1796. Coshocton County Chamber of Commerce, 124 Chestnut St., Coshocton, OH 43812; (614) 622–5411.

Miles & Directions

- 0.0 Ride north from the free public parking lot on 5th St.
- 0.1 Right on Chestnut St., which becomes County 16.
- 6.5 Left on Rte. 93 in the town of West Lafayette, where you'll find restaurants, a grocery, and convenience stores.
- 7.9 Straight across U.S. Hwy. 36 onto Rte. 93.
- 19.2 Proceed straight in the village of Baltic, where you'll find a convenience store.

If you are riding the 41.3-mile route, turn left on Rte. 651. At mile 25.2 turn left on Rte. 643 in the village of New Bedford, and pick up the directions below at mile 62.9.

- 25.1 Left on Rte. 39.
- 30.1 Right on Rte. 515 at the village of Walnut Creek, where you'll find several restaurants.
- 35.6 Right on U.S. Hwy. 62. **Use caution, and ride on the paved shoulder because significant traffic may be encountered.**
- 36.4 Left on Winesburg Rd. in the village of Winesburg, where you'll find restaurants and convenience stores.
- 41.2 Left on Bunkerhill Rd. in the village of Mt. Hope, where you'll find a grocery.

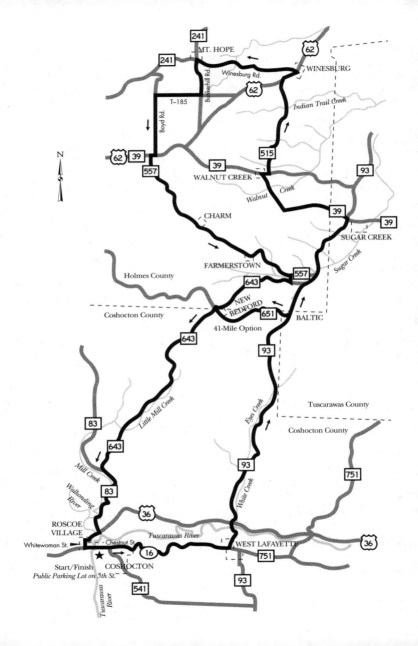

- 43.0 Right on T–185.
- 45.1 Left on Boyd Rd.
- 48.1 Right on U.S. Hwy. 62/Rte. 39, where you'll find a restaurant. **Use caution, and ride on the paved shoulder because significant traffic may be encountered.**
- 48.3 Left on Rte. 557.
- 52.8 Proceed straight on Rte. 557 in the village of Charm, where you'll find a restaurant.
- 55.8 Proceed straight on Rte. 557 in the village of Farmerstown, where you'll find a convenience store.
- 58.4 Right on Rte. 643.
- 58.8 Right on Rte. 643.
- 62.9 Proceed straight on Rte. 643 in the village of New Bedford, where you'll find a convenience store.
- 73.3 Left on Rte. 83.
- 77.1 Right on U.S. Hwy. 36. **Use caution and ride on the paved shoulder because significant traffic may be encountered.**
- 77.6 Right on Whitewoman St.
- 77.7 Left on Whitewoman St. in the Roscoe Village restoration, where you'll find several restaurants and an ice cream shop.
- 78.1 Left on Chestnut St. in the city of Coshocton.
- 78.9 Right on 5th St.
- 79.0 Arrive at the public parking lot.

34

River Rendezvous Challenge

When Roger and Bessey Kalter married in 1982, they decided it would be nice to honeymoon on a bicycle. After five and a half years, thirty-one countries, and more than 27,000 miles of pedaling, they were back home in Marietta. "It was much less expensive than our normal way of life," Roger said. "We sold our cars before we left and scrimped on accommodations as we traveled. My mom, Mildred, sold 400 subscriptions to a newsletter called *World Tour* that we sent back."

Talk about creative financing! Today the Kalters share their love of bicycling by organizing the River Rendezvous tour with the Marietta Rowing & Cycling Club. Held the first weekend of June, it's run as a two-day, out-and-back tour on a route that traces the Muskingum River between Duncan Falls and Marietta.

The Muskingum was made into a navigable river in 1842, when locks were built along its length. The locks still work today. At one time they linked the Ohio River with Lake Erie. Your starting point at Duncan Falls is at the site of lock no. 10, on the Muskingum Parkway.

Heading south you'll find heavily wooded, rural scenery punctuated with occasional farmsteads. At one time the valley was the nation's biggest producer of tomatoes. And, of course, the winding Muskingum River presents bicyclists with new views around each bend. The river is popular for boating, and ten sternwheel paddleboats operate on this stretch of the Muskingum. Buzzards soar over the river bluffs, and the bald eagle and great blue heron are seen more and more these days.

The first town of any consequence is Malta, sister town to Mc-Connelsville, just across the river. The towns are architectural gems that look little different from when Morgan's Raiders rode through during the Civil War on one of the few Confederate incursions into northern territory.

At Stockport you're a little over halfway, and you might consider lunch at the Riverside Restaurant, which looks out on the river and locks. Save dessert for Beverly, where you'll find Roger's Restaurant, featuring a 1950s-vintage ice cream parlor.

Between Beverly and Lowell you'll move away from the river and tackle some steep grades on hills about 150 feet higher than the river. You'll pass on the south side of the river from Lowell. If you're still hungry, or just curious, you can cross the bridge into Lowell, where you'll find restaurants, ice cream shops, and Buzzard's Bar, whose owner is known as a crusty character who fits the tavern's name.

You'll ride back along the Muskingum for most of the remaining distance to Marietta. **Use caution because there are a number of sharp-angled railroad crossings on this stretch.**

Marietta was named after Marie Antoinette by grateful Revolutionary War officers who were given land at the junction of the Ohio and Muskingum for back pay. We aren't taught this in school, but there were more French soldiers under Lafayette's command fighting the British at Yorktown than there were Americans under General Washington. The veterans settled at Marietta in 1788, and the town claims to have more Revolutionary War officers buried in Mound Cemetery than any other place in the country.

Your entry into Marietta will be marked by the sight of four steamboats. The *W.P. Snyder, Jr.* is the last steam-powered paddle wheeler and is part of the Ohio River Museum. The *Becky Thatcher* is a showboat and restaurant. The *Valley Gem* takes up to 300 people on excursion cruises on the Muskingum and Ohio rivers, including a special tour for riders on the annual River Rendezvous. The nearby *Claire-E* serves as a bed and breakfast.

The Basics

Start: Park at the Muskingum River Parkway Lock, 2 blocks south of the village of Duncan Falls on Rte. 60.

Length: 67.7 miles.

Terrain: Flat to gently rolling, with a few hills.

Food: In Duncan Falls there are a restaurant, a grocery, and a Dairy Queen. Convenience stores are all you'll find in Gaysport and Eagleport. In Malta and in McConnelsville, just off-route across the river, there are restaurants and groceries. At Stockport the Riverside Restaurant is recommended, as is Roger's Restaurant and ice cream parlor in Beverly. There is a restaurant in Waterford and a restaurant and ice cream shop off-route in Lowell. There are numerous restaurants and groceries in Marietta.

For more information: Marietta Rowing & Cycling Club, c/o Roger Kalter, P.O. Box 1081, Marietta, OH 45750; (614) 373–1784. Marietta/Washington County Convention & Visitors Bureau, 316 3rd St., Marietta, OH 45750; (614) 373–5178 or (800) 288–2577.

Bicycle service: In Marietta.

Miles & Directions

- 0.0 Head south on Rte. 60 from the parking area at the Muskingum River Parkway Lock. **Use caution on Rte. 60 because significant traffic may be present.**
- 4.8 Right onto County 2 across the Muskingum River in the village of Gaysport, where you'll find a convenience store.
- 11.3 Proceed straight onto Hwy. 699 in the village of Eagleport, where you'll find a convenience store.
- 18.9 Continue straight on Hwy. 699 in the village of Malta, where you'll find a restaurant and grocery.
- 29.0 Left on Hwy. 266 in the village of Stockport, where you'll find the Riverside Restaurant.

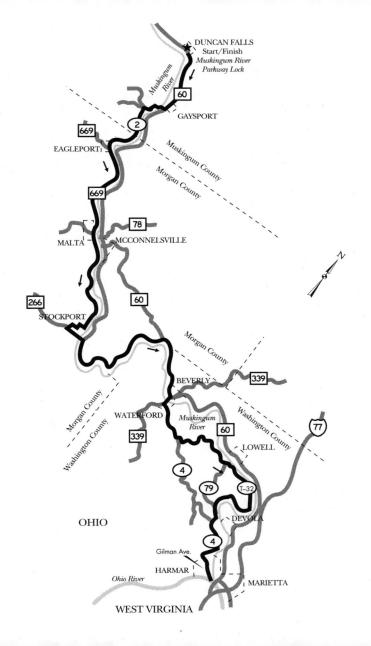

DUNCAN FALLS
Start/Finish
*Muskingum River
Parkway Lock*

60

GAYSPORT

669

2

EAGLEPORT

Muskingum River

669

Muskingum County

Morgan County

78

MALTA

McCONNELSVILLE

266

60

STOCKPORT

Morgan County

BEVERLY

339

Morgan County

Washington County

WATERFORD

Muskingum River

60

339

LOWELL

77

4

79

T-32

Washington County

DEVOLA

OHIO

4

Gilman Ave.

HARMAR

Ohio River

MARIETTA

N

WEST VIRGINIA

- 40.0 Right on Hwy. 60.
- 45.0 Right on Hwy. 339 in the town of Beverly, where you'll find Roger's Restaurant and ice cream parlor.
- 45.3 Left on County 4.
- 48.8 Left on County 60.
- 54.8 Right on T–32.
- 62.4 Left on County 79.
- 62.6 Left on County 4, which becomes Gilman Ave. in Marietta.
- 67.3 Left on Putnam Ave.
- 67.5 Left on Front St.
- 67.7 Arrive at City Park.

Wisconsin

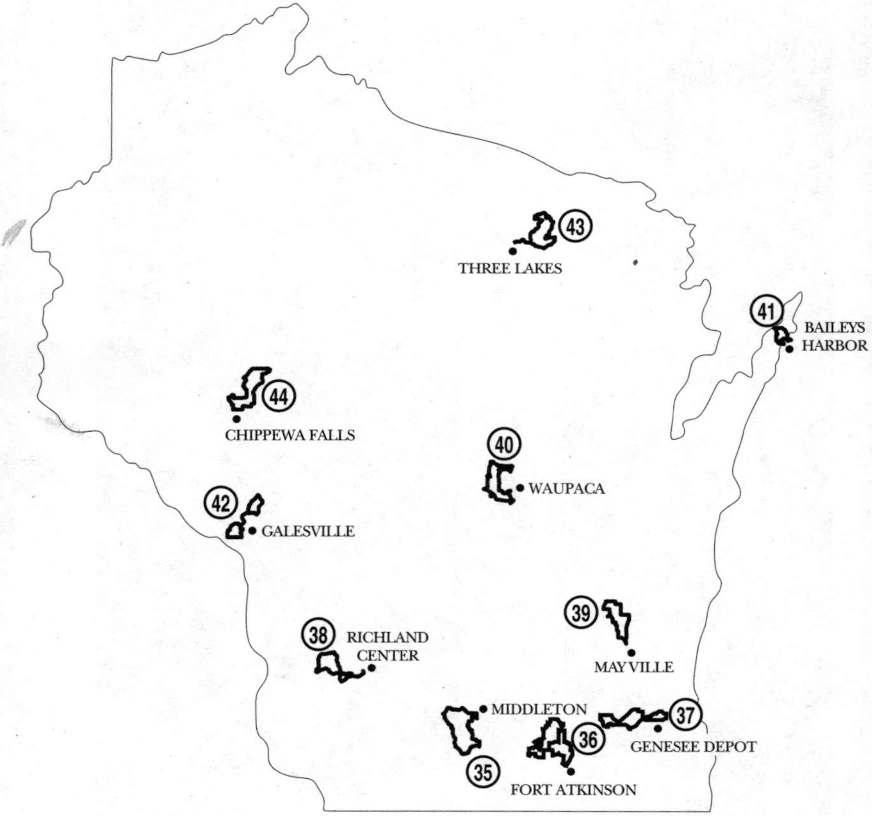

43
THREE LAKES
41
BAILEYS
HARBOR
44
CHIPPEWA FALLS
40
WAUPACA
42
GALESVILLE
39
38
RICHLAND
CENTER
MAYVILLE
MIDDLETON
37
36
GENESEE DEPOT
35
FORT ATKINSON

Wisconsin

35

Swiss Scene Classic

Madison's Bombay Bicycle Club is very active, organizing several well-publicized rides each week. The Swiss Scene route is one of three that are rotated for the club's annual century ride, which takes place in late September.

When Wisconsin was being settled in the mid-nineteenth century, it was a good time to leave nearly any European country. The diverse influx of immigrants made the state a real ethnic stew. You won't find such a mix of nationalities elsewhere in the United States, and this tour will take you through three towns with different ethnic flavors.

Mt. Horeb has a Norwegian character. The townsfolk even nicknamed their Main Street "the Trollway." Schubert's Cafe on Main Street is a great place to take a break. The town is very receptive to bicyclists. The Military Ridge State Trail runs through Mt. Horeb and brings more and more recreational riders in each year.

New Glarus is a picture-postcard-perfect Swiss village. The original settlers named it after their Old Country home in Glarus. Their descendants have built upon this heritage and made New Glarus into a very pleasant place, with a definite European flavor. You've got a number of food options in town, but be sure to try an order of *rosti* potatoes on the veranda of the New Glarus Hotel. The bakery across the street is also highly recommended. New Glarus is at the north end of the Sugar River State Trail, and bicyclists are a common sight in town.

Belleville was settled by French immigrants, and you'll see French names and distinctive gravestones in the local cemeteries. Other than some place-names like Lac Belle View, there isn't much evidence of French heritage. Still, it's a friendly little town, with a restaurant that serves good pies.

The ride also shows you the different character of glaciated and unglaciated terrain. On the eastern half of the loop, you'll ride over land that was covered by the thick ice sheet of the last continental glacier. The hills were rounded by the ice and lend themselves to farming. Dividing the two regions are high, rounded hills that run in parallel bands. These are the terminal moraines, the piles that mark the glacier's final push.

The western half of the route is in what's called the "Driftless Area," which was left untouched. The valleys are steep-sided and often wooded. Farms are tucked into valley niches or are on the rolling ridgetops. Hills are long and steep, as the process of erosion has had aeons longer to shape the land.

The unglaciated countryside is a favorite of bicyclists who don't mind a challenge. The valleys wind along and always surprise you with a lovely view as you round a bend. This route has some of the finest, including Spring Valley, on the way to Mazomanie; the valleys of Blue Mound, Elvers, and Moen creeks, on the way to Mt. Horeb; and Britt Valley, between Mt. Horeb and New Glarus.

The crossroads village of Paoli is probably the most popular bicycling destination in the area. Its short (15-mile) distance from Madison has a lot to do with that, but whatever the reason the beautiful old stone mill and town square are seldom without a few cyclists resting in the shade or filling their bottles at the water pump.

The Basics

Start: Park at Lakeview Park on County Q in Middleton, 0.75 mile north of University Ave., which is the main east-west street between Middleton and Madison.

Length: 99.1 miles.

Terrain: Rolling to hilly.

Food: Expect long stretches with no services. All the towns you pass through, except Ashton Corners and Paoli (where there are only taverns), have comfortable cafes and root beer or ice cream stands, in addition to groceries and convenience stores. There is a fine bakery in New Glarus.

For more information: Bombay Bicycle Club, P.O. Box 1454, Madison, WI 53701-0454. Greater Madison Convention & Visitors Bureau, 121 W. Doty St., Madison, WI 53703; (608) 255–0701.
Bicycle service: In Middleton, Mt. Horeb, New Glarus, and Verona.

Miles & Directions

- 0.0 Ride north on the bike path in Lakeview Park.
- 0.2 Left on Maywood Ave.
- 0.3 Right on Amherst Ave.
- 0.6 Left on County M (Century Ave.).
- 0.9 Right on Pheasant Branch Rd.
- 3.4 Left on County K.
- 5.9 Straight in the village of Ashton, where you'll find a tavern.
- 12.5 Left on Schuman Rd.
- 13.0 Right on Spring Valley Rd.
- 18.7 Right on County F.
- 18.9 Left on Carter Rd.
- 20.5 Right on Hwy. 78.
- 20.8 Left on Hudson St. into the town of Mazomanie, where you'll find a cafe, grocery, and root beer stand.
- 22.2 Left on Crocker St.
- 22.6 Right on Whitechapel St.
- 22.7 Left on Reeve Rd. **Use caution on the steep, winding downhill.**
- 26.8 Left on County FF.
- 28.5 Straight onto County F.
- 30.9 Left on County J.
- 32.8 Right on Bohn Rd.
- 34.1 Left on County JG. As you finish the steep climb in Stewart Park, you enter the town of Mt. Horeb, and County JG becomes Lake St.
- 38.2 Left on Wilson St.
- 38.3 Right on County JG (Washington St.).
- 38.5 Left on Main St. (U.S. Hwy. 18/151) in Mt. Horeb, where you'll find several restaurants and groceries.

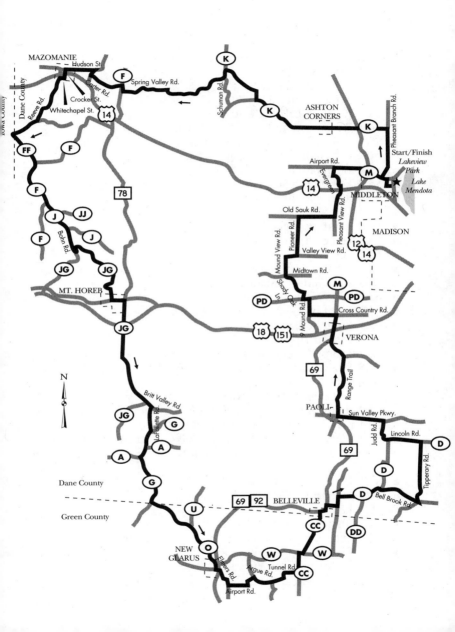

- 38.8 Straight on Main St. at Yap's House of Tailoring, where U.S. Hwy. 18/151 veers left.
- 39.0 Right on County JG (8th St.).
- 44.8 Left on Britt Valley Rd.
- 45.1 Right on LaFollette Rd.
- 46.4 Right on County G, which becomes County O.
- 55.1 Left on 4th Ave. in the town of New Glarus, where you'll find restaurants, groceries, and a bakery.
- 55.2 Right on Railroad St.
- 55.3 Left on 6th St.
- 55.6 Right on Elmers Rd.
- 56.4 Left on Airport Rd.
- 57.9 Right on Argue Rd.
- 58.8 Left on Tunnel Rd.
- 60.3 Left on County CC.
- 63.7 Right on Hwy. 69/92 (Main St.) in the town of Belleville, where you'll find restaurants and groceries.
- 63.9 Left on Hwy. 69 (River St.).
- 64.2 Right on County D.
- 67.1 Right on Bell Brook Rd.
- 69.1 Left on Tipperary Rd.
- 72.2 Left on Lincoln Rd., which becomes County D.
- 73.8 Straight on Lincoln where County D turns left. Lincoln becomes Judd Rd.
- 75.1 Left on Sun Valley Pkwy.
- 77.2 Right on Range Trail in the village of Paoli, where you'll find a tavern and, in the town park, a water pump.
- 80.3 Left on County M, which takes you into the town of Verona, where you'll find restaurants, groceries, and a root beer stand.
- 83.4 Left on Cross Country Rd.
- 84.7 Right on 9 Mound Rd.
- 85.4 Left on County PD.
- 85.7 Right on Shady Oak Ln.
- 87.2 Left on Midtown Rd.
- 87.5 Right on Mound View Rd.
- 88.5 Right on Valley View Rd.

- 89.0 Left on Pioneer Rd.
- 91.0 Right on Old Sauk Rd.
- 92.6 Left on Pleasant View Rd. **Use caution crossing U.S. Hwy. 14.**
- 94.3 Left on University Green.
- 94.4 Right on Evergreen Rd.
- 95.8 Right on Airport Rd., which becomes Century Ave.
- 98.5 Right on Amherst Ave.
- 98.8 Left on Maywood Ave.
- 98.9 Right on the bike path.
- 99.1 Arrive at Lakeview Park.

36

Tour de Fort Cruise

When you trace the quiet country roads of the Tour de Fort route you cover more than gently rolling, scenic dairy farmland. Before the settlers arrived the area had all the attributes Native Americans needed for an ideal home. A mix of prairie, woods, marshland, lakes, and rivers was rich with game, fish, and edible and medicinal plants. Foot trails crisscrossed the area. The Crawfish and Rock rivers were natural canoe routes.

On the third Sunday of August, a typical turnout of 700-plus cyclists sets out to explore the scenic countryside on the Tour de Fort. Some may opt for a 15-mile route offered in additon to the 62- and 35 mile routes shown here.

The history of Native Americans in pre-Columbian times is shrouded in mystery. Among the tantilizing clues from their cultures are the earthen mounds they left behind. Evidence of one of these enigmatic groups is along this route.

Rolling north past Wisconsin dairy farms, you'll visit Aztalan State Park, one of the state's most significant archaeological sites. Flat-topped, pyramid-shaped mounds mark it as an outpost of the Middle Mississippian Culture, a vast trading network centered near St. Louis. Lacking modern dating techniques, early scientists theorized that Aztalan was the homeland of the Aztecs. The Mississipians traded items like obsidian from the Rocky Mountains, copper from the Lake Superior area, and shells from the Gulf Coast. Thriving for more than 300 years, the fortified town was destroyed by fire before the time of Columbus. The nearby Aztalan Museum exhibits pioneer artifacts, preserves three log cabins and has an observation tower overlooking the park.

A mystery of a different sort has surrounded Rock Lake since the last century. Low water and, recently, scuba diving have supposedly revealed underwater stone pyramids. Speculation about their builders ranges from Aztecs, to Canary Islanders, to survivors of the lost continent of Atlantis. I wouldn't lose any sleep over it if I were you.

If you are riding the long loop, the route will take you through the picturesque village of Cambridge, a good place for a restaurant or bakery stop. Just beyond, in Rockdale, there is a fine view of the old mill dam from the bridge over the Koshkonong Creek.

The Basics

Start: Park at Jones Park on 6th St. several blocks south of the Rock River on Business Hwy. 26 (Janesville Ave.) in Fort Atkinson.
Length: 34.7 or 62.2 miles.
Terrain: Flat to gently rolling.
Food: There are groceries, bakeries, convenience stores, and numerous restaurants in Fort Atkinson, Jefferson, and Cambridge. In Lake Mills a cafe and grocery are off-route. In Aztalan and Rockdale you'll find taverns. There is a restaurant on Lake Ripley.
For more information: Tour de Fort Metric Century, c/o Gary Gramley, #6 Milwaukee Ave. E., Fort Atkinson, WI 53538; (414) 563–5279. Fort Atkinson Area Chamber of Commerce, 244 N. Main St., Fort Atkinson, WI 53538-1829; (414) 563–3210. Cambridge Chamber of Commerce, 137 Main St., P.O. Box 330, Cambridge, WI 53523-0330; (608) 423–3780.
Bicycle service: Off-route in Lake Mills.

Miles & Directions

- 0.0 Right out of Jones Park on S. 6th St. followed by an imme diate left on Grove St.
- 0.3 Left on S. 3rd St. followed by an immediate right on Robert St.
- 1.3 Right on Cramer St.

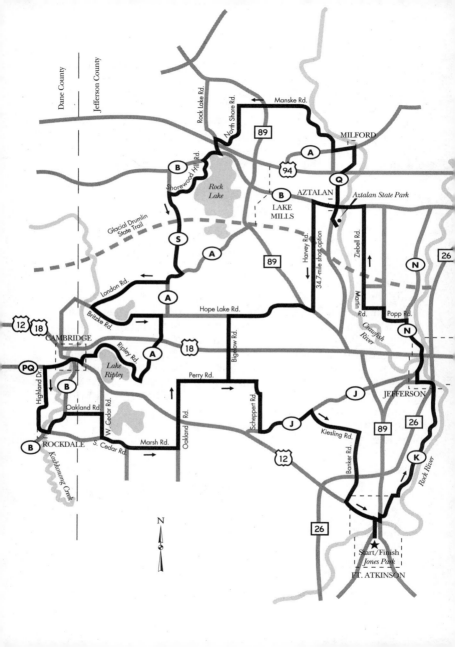

- 1.9 Left on Jefferson St.
- 2.1 Right on Blackhawk Dr.
- 2.2 Left on Hwy. 26 (High St.).
- 2.3 Right on County K.
- 5.8 Left on Collins Rd.
- 5.9 Straight across Hwy. 26 at the south end of the town of Jefferson, where you'll find several restaurants.
- 6.4 Right on Hillside Dr.
- 6.9 Right on Wisconsin Ave.
- 7.1 Straight on Wisconsin Ave. at River Front Park, where you'll find water, restrooms, and a picnic area.
- 7.4 Left on W. Linden Dr. (S. Copland goes straight).
- 7.5 Right on S. Pleasant Ave.
- 8.2 Left on W. Clark St. Clark becomes Hyer Dr. and County N.
- 8.8 Left on Popp Rd.
- 10.3 Left on Martin Rd. Martin Rd. becomes Popp Rd. again.
- 11.6 Straight on Popp Rd.
- 13.4 Left on Ziebell Rd.
- 14.2 Left on County B.
- 15.1 Left on County Q at the unincorporated village of Aztalan, where you'll find a tavern and soft drink machine.
- 15.3 Left into Aztalan State Park, where you'll find water and restrooms.
- 15.6 Turn around at lower parking lot and return to park entrance.
- 15.9 Right out of park on County Q

If you are riding the 34.7-mile route, turn left on County B at mile 16.1 in the village of Aztalan. At mile 16.8 turn left on Harvey Rd. At mile 20.3 turn right on Hwy. 89. At mile 20.6 turn left on Hope Lake Rd. At mile 21.2 ride straight on Hope Lake Rd. At mile 22.8 turn left on Bigelow Rd. (becomes Kreklow Rd.). At mile 24.8 turn left on Scheppert Rd. From here pick up the directions below at mile 54.7.

- 16.1 Straight on County Q.
- 18.2 Left on County A in the unincorporated village of Milford.

- 18.9 Right on Manske Rd.
- 21.9 Straight across Hwy. 89 onto Woodland Rd.
- 22.6 Left on North Shore Rd.
- 24.6 Left on Rock Lake Rd.
- 24.8 Right on County B.
- 25.5 Left on Shorewood Hill Rd.
- 27.5 Left on County S.
- 30.1 Right on County A.
- 30.6 Right on London Rd.
- 33.1 Left on Britzke Rd.
- 33.9 Straight onto Hope Lake Rd.
- 35.5 Right on County A.
- 37.5 Right on Ripley Rd.
- 39.3 Left on Park Rd.
- 39.6 Right on Church Rd.
- 39.9 Left on Potters St., which becomes North St. in the village of Cambridge, where you'll find several restaurants, a bakery, and a convenience store.
- 40.4 Left on Mill St.
- 40.5 Right on Main St. followed by an immediate left on Water St., which becomes County PQ.
- 41.3 Left on Highland Dr.
- 42.9 Straight on Jones St. at Koshkonong Dr.
- 43.4 Left on Adams St.
- 43.5 Left on County B in the unincorporated village of Rockdale, where you'll find a tavern.
- 44.2 Right on Oakland Rd.
- 45.4 Right on W. Cedar Rd.
- 46.2 Left on S. Cedar Rd.
- 47.1 Left on Marsh Rd.
- 48.6 Left on Oakland Rd.
- 50.7 Right on Perry Rd.
- 52.3 Straight on Scheppert Rd.
- 54.7 Left on County J.
- 56.4 Right on Kiesling Rd.
- 58.0 Right on Banker Rd.
- 60.3 Left on Cramer St.

- 60.9 Right on Robert St.
- 61.9 Left on S. 3rd St. followed by an immediate right on Grove St.
- 62.2 Right on S. 6th St. followed by an immediate left to arrive at Jones Park.

37

Rolling Around
Rome Cruise

Depending on how you look at it, the myth is greater than the reality. Rome, Wisconsin, gained some notoriety as kind of a Peyton Place with cows on the recent TV series *Picket Fences*. In reality, Rome is tiny, unexciting, and much nicer than its TV cousin. In early June, Cream City Bicycle Club riders from Milwaukee leave their urban home base for a look at the real Rome. In the process of covering this 42-mile route they ride over some of the loveliest farm and wood land in the state.

The starting point, at Town of Genesee Park, has yet another acting connection. Nestled in the trees just to the east along Depot Road is Ten Chimneys, former home of Alfred Lunt and Lynn Fontanne. Lunt and Fontanne were the toast of Broadway in the 1930s. They chose to spend their free time and retirement in the beautiful rolling hills of the kettle moraine, and many famous film and stage stars, including Laurence Olivier, visited there. Wow, that's a lot of fame for a couple of unincorporated towns and one bike tour.

Heading east from Genesee Depot you'll pedal over the kettle moraine, jumbled terrain left by the rubbing together of two great ice sheets of the last continental glacier. The wooded hills to the south are part of the Kettle Moraine State Forest. Beyond, the terrain becomes a mix of marshland and flat to rolling farmland.

With the exception of a few miles of riding through newly built housing, the region is remarkably rural despite the popularity of Waukesha County as a bedroom-community for Milwaukee. You'll even miss the small business districts of Dousman and Wales on this route. A stop for water between the towns at the flowing artesian well on Parry Road should make up for it. Artesian wells flow constantly because they lie at low spots and the water table is higher in the surrounding hills. This well is still popular with the locals, who often stop to fill jugs with the clean, cold water.

There are enough twists and turns along the route to make you believe that all roads lead to Rome. Enjoy your visit there, but don't take any bets that it wasn't built in a day.

The Basics

Start: Town of Genesee Park 0.5 mile west of Hwy. 83 on Depot Rd. in the village of Genesee Depot.
Length: 41.5 miles.
Terrain: Gently rolling to moderately hilly.
Food: There are water and restrooms at Town of Genesee Park and restaurants in the village of Genesee Depot. In Rome there are several taverns. In Dousman there are a grocery, a cafe, and a tavern 0.5 mile north of the ride route on Main St.
For more information: Cream City Bicycle Club, P.O. Box 894, Milwaukee, WI 53201; (414) 476–1020, box 50. Waukesha Area Tourism Council, 223 Wisconsin Ave., Waukesha, WI 53186-4926; (414) 542–0330 or (800) 366–8474.
Bicycle service: In Wales and nearby in Oconomowoc, Delafield, and Waukesha.

Miles & Directions

- 0.0 Right out of Town of Genesee Park on Depot Rd.
- 0.1 Right on Highview Rd.
- 0.6 Left on County D.
- 3.9 Left on County C and County D.
- 4.2 Straight on County C where County D goes to the right.
- 6.4 Straight on County CI.
- 7.6 Right on County ZC.
- 10.0 Straight on County Z.
- 10.4 Straight on Northey Rd. at Waukesha/Jefferson County line.
- 12.6 Right on County E followed by an immediate left on Lundt Rd.

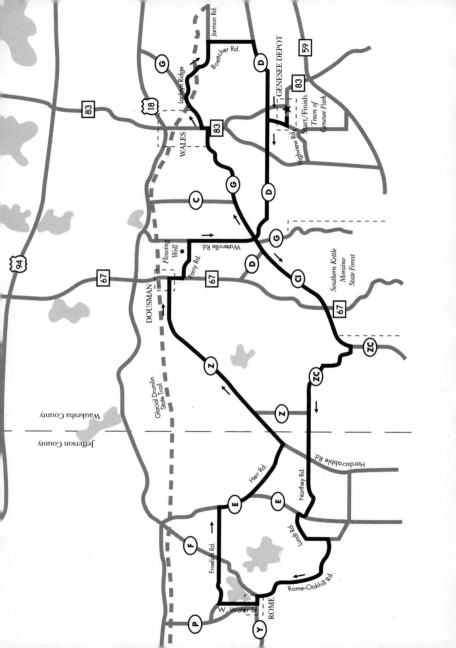

- 13.9 Right on Rome-Oakhill Rd.
- 16.7 Left off of Rome-Oakhill Rd. on County F (Main St.) into the village of Rome, where you'll find several taverns.
- 16.9 Right on W. Water St.
- 17.8 Right on Froelich Rd.
- 20.4 Continue straight across County F on Froelich Rd.
- 21.3 Right on County E.
- 22.9 Left on Herr Rd.
- 24.0 Left on Hardscrabble Rd.
- 27.5 Straight on County Z (unmarked). County Z becomes W. Ottawa St. in the village of Dousman, where you'll find a tavern and grocery 0.5 mile north of the route on Main St.
- 28.4 Right on Hwy. 67.
- 28.8 Left on Parry Rd.
- 29.7 Straight. Drinking water available at flowing well on left side of road at bottom of hill.
- 29.9 Right on County C (Waterville Rd.).
- 31.6 Left on County C and County D followed by an immediate left on County C where County D splits off to the right.
- 32.7 Straight on County G (Brandy Brook Rd.) where County C turns to the left.
- 35.0 Left on Hwy. 83.
- 35.1 Right on County G (Brandy Brook Rd.) into the village of Wales.
- 35.8 Straight at unnamed town street (bicycle service is located several blocks to the left on this street).
- 35.9 Right on Lochtyn Ridge.
- 36.9 Right on Boettcher Rd.
- 37.7 Right on County GD (Boettcher Rd.) where Jarmon Rd. goes straight.
- 38.9 Right on County D.
- 39.2 **Use caution crossing railroad tracks.**
- 40.6 Straight across Hwy. 83 on County D.
- 40.9 Left on Highview Rd.
- 41.4 Left on Depot Rd.
- 41.5 Left into Town of Genesee Park.

38

Ocooch Mountain Challenge

Here's a tour to take on once you've gotten your climbing legs in shape. You'll have to tackle four steep, 400-foot climbs to cover the whole route. It's all part of the plan. The annual Ocooch Mountain Fall Bike Tour was designed with challenge in mind. It takes place on the first weekend of October in conjunction with Richland Center's apple harvest festival, Centerfest, and the tour also features shorter 12- and 35-mile loops. This is a time of year when cyclists usually have a decent conditioning base. Bring on the mountains.

OK, 400-foot hills aren't exactly mountains, but they've been called the Ocooch Mountains since the earliest explorers came through, and the climbs are steep enough to make your muscles feel like they are. The first uphill grind comes early as you turn up County Y and Premo Hill Road. At the top you'll find Scholl's Orchard Store. It's a great place to buy a snack or two, but skip picking up a bag of apples—you'd regret hauling the extra weight.

The orchard is the last place to take on food or water for a long distance. You're in for a long, high-speed downhill run into the valley of Mill Creek on County Q. The valley scenery is hard to beat along County E. Late in the last century, a complete mastodon skeleton was found in this valley. Other than the farms the surroundings probably didn't look a lot different when the animal was alive. This area was spared the leveling hand of all four great continental glaciers of the last million years. Hence the steep hills.

Highway 171 takes you along Core Hollow and into the second climb, on County UU. One section is so steep that if you can stay on your bike, you deserve a medal. Soon you'll be screaming down into Knapp Creek Valley, which will lead you north to your third climb of the day, on County U. Next you'll have a long valley run southward along Mill Creek, before turning uphill again after Boaz.

The last downhill run takes you back to Richland Center, which is worth spending some time exploring. Its historic downtown area retains the character of its nineteenth-century origin. A truly exceptional building is the Warehouse, designed by Frank Lloyd Wright in 1915. It's a rare example of his work in the period when he designed the Imperial Hotel in Tokyo. Wright was born in Richland Center in 1867, and the once purely functional Warehouse now houses a museum about the architect and a tea room.

The Basics

Start: Park at the University of Wisconsin–Richland campus, just west of Richland Center on U.S. Hwy. 14.
Length: 47.3 miles.
Terrain: Flat, rolling, and very hilly.
Food: Many options in Richland Center; Scholl's Orchard Store on Premo Hill Rd.; the Boaz Country Store, at the junction of County E and U.S. Hwy. 14; and a tavern and a town park with water in the village of Boaz.
For more information: Ocooch Mountain Fall Bicycle Tour, c/o Richland Medical Center, 1313 W. Seminary St., Richland Center, WI 53581; (608) 647–6161. Richland Area Chamber of Commerce, 170 W. Seminary St., P.O. Box 128, Richland Center, WI 53581; (608) 647–6205.
Bicycle service: In Richland Center.

Miles & Directions

- 0.0 Ride south from the University of Wisconsin–Richland campus parking lot.
- 0.1 Proceed straight across U.S. Hwy. 14 onto W. Side Dr. **Caution: Heavy traffic may be encountered.**

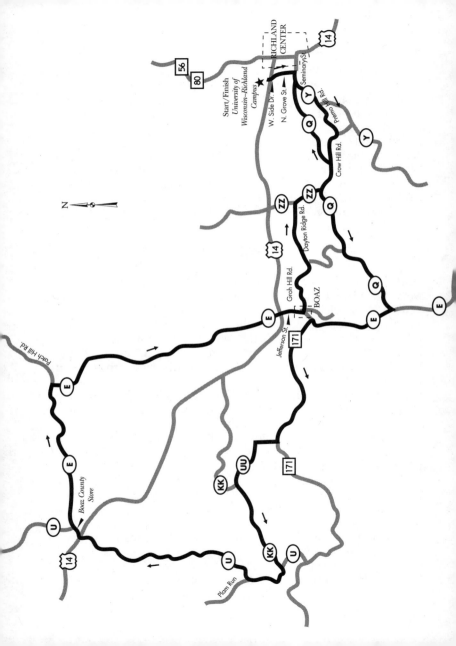

- 0.5 Bear right at N. Grove St.
- 0.9 Right on Seminary St.
- 1.2 Left on County Y.
- 2.1 Right on Premo Hill Rd., which becomes Crow Hill Rd.
- 4.0 Left on County Q.
- 8.8 Right on County E.
- 11.2 Left on Hwy. 171.
- 15.1 Right on County UU.
- 17.2 Left on County KK.
- 19.8 Right on County U.
- 26.5 Left on U.S. Hwy. 14. **Caution: Ride on the paved shoulder because significant traffic may be encountered.**
- 26.6 Right on County E.
- 38.2 Proceed straight across U.S. Hwy. 14 onto County E. You'll find the Boaz Country Store at this intersection.
- 38.7 Bear left on Jefferson St. next to Harris Lumber in the village of Boaz, where you'll find a tavern and a town park with water.
- 38.8 Left on Jefferson St. next to the Lonesome Dove Tavern. Jefferson St. becomes Groh Hill Rd.
- 40.3 Left on Dayton Ridge Rd.
- 42.0 Right on County ZZ.
- 42.9 Left on County Q, which becomes Seminary St.
- 46.5 Left on N. Grove St.
- 46.8 Bear left onto W. Side Dr.
- 47.2 Proceed straight across U.S. Hwy. 14.
- 47.3 Arrive at the University of Wisconsin–Richland campus.

39

Audubon Days Ramble

John James Audubon would have liked Horicon Marsh. As he roamed the frontier of the United States in the early nineteenth century, Audubon often found vast, wild places filled with wonderful birds to paint and write about. The country has changed, and such havens are becoming fewer. Today there aren't many that can match the expanse of the Horicon National Wildlife Refuge.

Nearby Mayville is the starting point for this route. It's one of three distances offered as part of the town's annual Audubon Days celebration, which is always held on the first weekend of October. It's a fun, small-town festival, featuring a variety of sports and entertainment, including a rubber duck race in the Rock River.

You'll leave Fireman's Field Park and wind through the quaint streets of Mayville. The country starts right at the edge of town (there aren't any burbs in Mayville). Soon you'll be rolling along the Niagara escarpment, the western edge of a vast sheet of limestone that stretches all the way to Niagara Falls. It cradles the marsh and offers the cyclist a high-ground perspective seldom found around these lush wetlands.

On a breezy day you can look over the marsh and watch the tall green cattail reeds roll like the waves on a sea. In fall and spring the air over the marsh will be alive with chevron formations of honking Canada geese and other birds. Each year they visit Horicon in the tens of thousands on their way to and from their nesting areas. Birds in flight are one of nature's greatest wonders. Bring a pair of binoculars and you'll soon be able to tell the disciplined formations of geese from those of the cranes and ducks.

Birds don't just pass through Horicon; they live there, too. A stop at the Horicon National Wildlife Refuge Headquarters, off County Z, will give you a chance to pick up some information on the wildlife in the marsh and the work of the refuge. The lookout at the headquarters is a good place to take a break.

The views don't end there. Farther north you'll turn west on Point Road and loop around close to the edge of the marsh. As you swing east and inland, you're likely to see more geese in the cornfields than over the marsh, at least in the fall. They flock to the fields after the harvest to glean the leavings. A field of geese taking flight at once is a sight to behold—and they're noisy, too!

Dairy farms highlight the scenery until you reach the village of LeRoy. You can see the steeple of St. Andrews Church for miles before you get to the village. In town you'll find a restaurant and tavern. From LeRoy it's a fast, easy roll back to Mayville on County V, the only road where you'll find any significant amount of traffic.

The Basics

Start: Fireman's Field Park, off County Y on the east side of Mayville. From Hwy. 28/67, cross the Rock River on Bridge St.
Length: 25.0 miles.
Terrain: Rolling.
Food: There are cafes and groceries in Mayville and a restaurant and tavern in LeRoy.
For more information: Audubon Days, Attn: Pauline Ellington, Mayville Chamber of Commerce, P.O. Box 185, Mayville, WI 53050; (414) 387–5776.
Bicycle service: In Mayville.

Miles & Directions

- 0.0 Ride north on Park St. in Fireman's Field Park.
- 0.1 Left on German St.
- 0.3 Left on Bridge St.
- 0.4 Right on Main St., where you'll find a cafe and a grocery store.
- 0.7 Left on Breckenridge St.

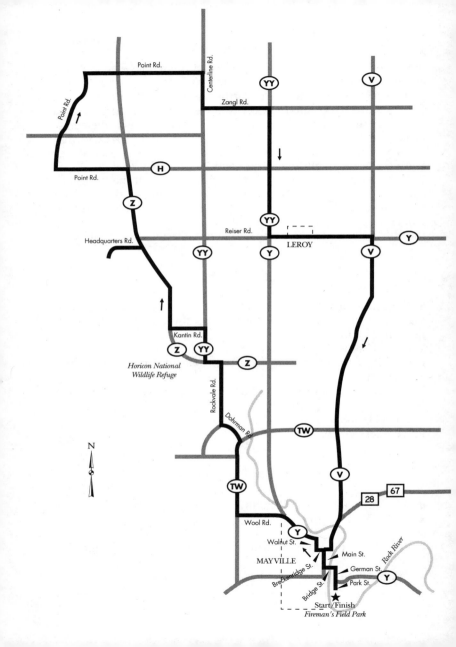

- 0.9 Right on Walnut St.
- 1.1 Left on County Y (Kekoskee St.).
- 1.7 Left on Wool Rd.
- 2.5 Right on County TW.
- 3.6 Left on Dohrman Rd.
- 4.0 Right on Rockvale Rd.
- 5.0 Left on County Z.
- 5.3 Right on County YY.
- 5.7 Left on Kantin Rd.
- 6.2 Right on County Z.
- 7.6 Left on Headquarters Rd. to the Horicon National Wildlife Refuge Headquarters.
- 8.1 Stop at the rest area and scenic overlook, turn around, and ride back out.
- 8.6 Left on County Z.
- 9.9 Left on Point Rd. at the junction with County H.
- 11.0 Right on Point Rd.
- 12.6 Straight across County Z.
- 14.1 Right on Centerline Rd.
- 14.9 Left on Zangl Rd.
- 15.9 Right on County YY.
- 17.9 Left on County Y at Reiser Rd. into the village of LeRoy, where you'll find a restaurant and tavern.
- 19.4 Right on County V.
- 22.4 Straight across County TW on County V.
- 23.8 Right on Hwy. 28/67 (Main St.).
- 24.8 Left on Bridge St.
- 24.9 Right on German St.
- 25.0 Right on Park St.; arrive at Fireman's Field Park.

Hartman Creek Ramble

The quiet roads of Waupaca County are popular routes to pedal. The pavement is usually good, and the scenery varies from farmland to woods, from swift-running streams to clear blue lakes. The Chain O' Lakes area is vacationland Wisconsin-style, and relaxed hospitality is the word. Several tours use these roads, but this loop is part of one of the most popular: the Hartman Creek Metric Century, held on the first weekend of June.

Leaving the tall pines of Hartman Creek State Park, you'll head east on one of the prettiest roads in the state. Rural Road has been designated a State Rustic Road, thereby protecting it from development. You'll appreciate that as you glide past the Old Stagecoach Inn and other simple Greek Revival houses. The Crystal River twists through the tiny village of Rural. Wouldn't you like to live there, just to have a postmark that says RURAL, WISCONSIN?

Farther on the route follows the babbling Crystal River before turning north to the village of King. The State Veterans Home is the biggest thing in King. It was originally built to care for injured veterans of the Civil War. Several restaurants and taverns line the route in King. A local favorite is off the route, 0.25 mile farther north on County QQ. The Clearwater Harbor restaurant sits on the shore of the Chain O' Lakes, and its deck is a great place to watch the sunset. Excursion cruises of the lakes leave its dock on a regular schedule during the summer months.

As you leave the lakes area, you'll roll over the undulating terrain that is the legacy of the last continental glacier. It melted only about 10,000 years ago, and the rocky soil it left behind is not very good for farming. This makes for a pleasant mix of agriculture in suitable spots and woods everywhere else. You'll notice that roads are seldom straight and that streams twist and turn every which way. Ten thousand years is not a very long time for the forces of nature to erode what the glacier dumped. The result is bicycling that's never boring. There's always another scenic view around the next corner. Often that view is of a glacial lake like Hartman Lake, which is a great place to take a dip after your ride, by the way.

The Basics

Start: Park at the Hartman Lake shelter parking lot on E. Windfeldt Ln. in Hartman Creek State Park (admission required). The park is 2 miles south of Hwy. 54, 5 miles east of Waupaca.
Length: 31.0 miles.
Terrain: Flat to gently rolling.
Food: In Rural there is a grocery store 1 block north of the route. There are several restaurants on- or just off-route in the village of King. At the County Q Bridge across the Chain O' Lakes, there are a restaurant and an ice cream shop.
For more information: Harbor Bike, 112 S. Main St., Waupaca, WI 54981; (715) 258–5404. Waupaca Area Chamber of Commerce, 221 S. Main St., Waupaca, WI 54981; (715) 258–7343.
Bicycle service: In Waupaca.

Miles & Directions

- 0.0 Follow E. Windfeldt Ln. west from the Hartman Lake shelter parking lot.
- 0.2 Right at the stop sign. Follow the park road to the entrance.
- 0.8 Right on Rural Rd.
- 4.1 Continue straight across Hwy. 22 onto Potts Rd. into the village of Rural.
- 4.5 Proceed straight as Potts Rd. becomes Rural Rd. again.
- 4.8 Right on Sanders Rd.
- 5.2 Left on County K.
- 6.0 Left on Rural Rd. and across the bridge.

- 6.1 Right on Smith Rd.
- 7.4 Right on County QQ.
- 7.5 Continue straight across Hwy. 22 onto County QQ.
- 8.2 Left on Grandview Dr. in the village of King, where you'll find several restaurants.
- 9.8 Right on County Q.
- 10.2 Straight across the Chain O' Lakes Bridge, where you'll find a restaurant and an ice cream shop.
- 11.0 Follow County Q to the right.
- 12.0 Continue straight across Hwy. 54 onto County Q.
- 14.3 Continue straight across U.S. Hwy. 10 onto County Q.
- 14.9 Right on Larson Rd.
- 17.1 Left on Oakland Rd.
- 18.1 Left on Haase Rd.
- 20.8 Right on County Q.
- 21.0 Left on Grenlie Rd.
- 22.5 Left on N. Foley Rd.
- 23.4 Continue straight across U.S. Hwy. 10 onto S. Foley Rd.
- 25.2 Right on Cobbtown Rd.
- 25.8 Left on Townline Rd.
- 27.5 Proceed straight across Hwy. 54 onto Badger Rd.
- 28.7 Left on Edminster Rd.
- 30.2 Right on Hartman Creek Rd. into Hartman Creek State Park.
- 30.8 Left on E. Windfeldt Ln.
- 31.0 Arrive at Hartman Lake shelter parking lot.

41

Ride for Nature Ramble

The Ridges Sanctuary straddles a point that separates Baileys Harbor and Moonlight Bay. Seventeen sand ridges parallel the curve of Baileys Harbor. The oldest of these abandoned beach dunes dates back 2,400 years. Within these confines thrives a world of wildflowers with names like Trailing Arbutus, Arctic Primrose, Showy Lady Slipper, and Fringed Gentian. On the third Saturday of June each year, the Ridges Sanctuary hosts the Ride for Nature to support its work of preserving its unique heritage of a hundred flowering plants.

The tour starts at the town hall in Baileys Harbor, an old fishing port on the Lake Michigan shore of the Door County peninsula. Just north of town the route takes an out-and-back course along a beach road that separates the bay from the sanctuary. You may want to pause for a stroll through the wildflowers on one of the many sand-ridge trails.

There's more lake scenery along County Q as you skirt the shore of Moonlight Bay and take another side trip to the Cana Island Lighthouse and the sandy beaches of Spike Horn Bay. You may even recognize the spot's scenic isolation from published photos. Don't be shy. Set your camera's timer and get in the picture yourself. If you like, you can walk the short, rocky causeway to the lighthouse—visitors are welcome.

Back out on County Q, the route follows North Bay before heading west across the woods and farmland of the peninsula's interior. You're on a straight course for a fine overview of Eagle Harbor and the wooded bluffs and islands of Peninsula State Park. You'll descend into the town of Ephraim, as picture-perfect a collection of white church spires and clapboard homes as can be found in any New England village. Just 1 block north of the intersection of

County Q and Highway 42 is Wilson's restaurant, a Door County landmark since 1906. Its latest menu hit is a veggie sandwich, which makes for a light lunch to follow up with one of Wilson's ice cream sundaes while watching the windsurfers ply the waters of the bay across the road.

Retracing the route out of Ephraim, you'll use your low gears winding up the 150-foot bluff before turning south to follow quiet roads through the gently rolling orchards, farmland, and marshland back to Baileys Harbor.

The Basics

Start: Park at the Baileys Harbor Town Hall in Baileys Harbor.
Length: 28.6 miles.
Terrain: Flat to gently rolling.
Food: Several restaurants and groceries in Baileys Harbor and Ephraim.
For more information: Ride for Nature, c/o C. Schuster, 2912 Lake Forest Dr., Sturgeon Bay, WI 54235; (414) 743–8138, e-mail:cschuste@mail.wisnet.net. Door County Chamber of Commerce, P.O. Box 406, Sturgeon Bay, WI 54235; (414) 743–4456.
Bicycle service: Available nearby in Fish Creek.

Miles & Directions

- 0.0 Turn left on Hwy. 57 from Baileys Harbor Town Hall parking lot.
- 0.1 Right on Ridges Rd.
- 2.1 Turn around at the yacht club.
- 4.1 Right on Hwy. 57.
- 4.6 Right on County Q.
- 8.1 Right on Cana Island Rd.
- 10.4 Turn around at the end of the road.
- 12.7 Right on County Q.
- 17.8 Straight across Hwy. 57 onto County Q.

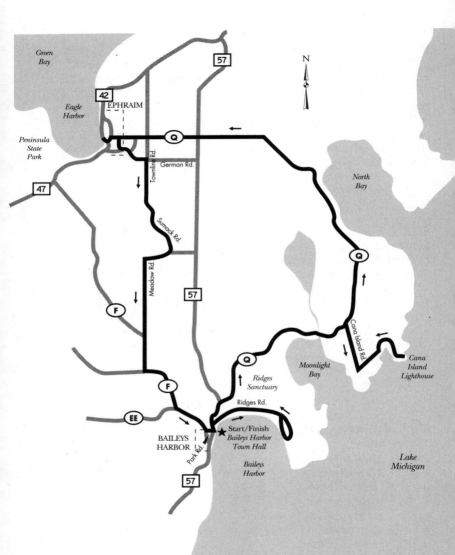

- 19.7 Left on County Q (Moravia St.) in the town of Ephraim.
- 19.8 Right at Hwy. 42 (Water St.).
- 19.9 Turn around at Wilson's restaurant and ice cream sundae shop.
- 20.1 Left on County Q.
- 20.2 Right on County Q.
- 20.5 Right on Norway St.
- 20.8 Left on German Rd.
- 21.4 Right on Townline Rd., which becomes Sumack Rd.
- 23.5 Right on Meadow Rd.
- 25.8 Straight onto County F.
- 27.8 Left to follow County F at the intersection with County EE.
- 28.5 Left on Park Rd.
- 28.6 Arrive at Baileys Harbor Town Hall.

42

Apple Affair Cruise

To the people who live in Galesville, the surrounding hills and orchards seem like the Garden of Eden. They certainly did for one local, the Reverend David O. Van Slyke. Before the turn of the century, he traveled the country lecturing that this land was the actual biblical site. Rattlesnakes live on the bluffs. Apples grow in the orchards. What more proof do you need?

Bicycling is the best way to enjoy the scenery that inspired Van Slyke. The first weekend of October, the town celebrates the orchard harvest with the Apple Affair, a town festival and bicycle tour. The town square is alive with polka music, orchard harvestings, and craft sales. You can even buy a slice of the world's biggest apple pie. These 15- and 41-mile routes are based on the annual tour. The short loop is basically flat, with one long climb. On the long route you'll cover most of that loop and add two more long climbs, plus the valleys of Beaver, Bear, and French creeks.

The first leg of either route heads south onto the broad floodplain of the nearby Mississippi River. This is the fertile farmland the Midwest is famous for. As you turn to the north, the wooded bluffs that line the wide valley loom ahead. It's in the narrow bluff clefts that you'll find the orchards of Galesville. Orchard stands in the area are open from mid-August to late October. Just a short distance off the route, on Grove Valley Road, Kaste's Orchard has a pick-your-own stand of easy-to-reach, dwarf apple trees.

As you pass through the orchards, a 2-mile, 300-foot climb on Sacia Road will give you a taste for the kind of grades you'll find in the area. The descent is steep and twisty. At the bottom you can decide to turn left and tackle more climbs and miles or head straight for a short run back into Galesville. If you go for the long route, you'll be treated to some of the loveliest valley scenery in the state.

Rolling north along the wide valley of Beaver Creek, the prosperous farms are set against the backdrop of wooded bluffs. At Frenchville, now just a collection of houses and a farm implement dealer, you'll cross the valley and begin a 2-mile, 250-foot climb of Peacock Hill on Dopp Road. Again, the descent is steep and twisty as you lose all that elevation in 1.5 miles. Your speed will propel you north into the valley of Bear Creek and to the town of Ettrick. The town's cafe and a convenience store are your only food options until you near Galesville.

North of Ettrick the valley begins to narrow before you recross U.S. Highway 53 and start a 200-foot climb on Kittleson Road. Just after the crest you'll turn south on County I for a long, glorious descent down the tight, wooded valley of French Creek. As the road flattens, you'll have another chance to enjoy Beaver Valley as you retrace County T back to Galesville.

Galesville is home to the Mill Road Cafe, widely noted for its vegetarian cooking, desserts, and entertainment ranging from folk music to jazz. The music is scheduled most weekends and some weekday evenings, but the food and desserts are waiting for you anytime.

The Basics

Start: The town square, at the corner of Ridge Ave. and U.S. Hwy. 53 (Main St.) in Galesville.

Length: 15.3 or 41.2 miles.

Terrain: Flat to very hilly.

Food: The Mill Road Cafe in Galesville is open for breakfast, lunch, and dinner seven days a week during the riding season. The Arctic Springs Supper Club on County T, 0.5 mile north of Sacia Road, is open for lunch and dinner. Apple orchards sell their fruit from mid-August through October. In the town of Ettrick, there are a cafe and a convenience store.

For more information: Mark Heal, Galesville Apple Affair Bike Tour, Box 214, Galesville, WI 54630; (608) 582–4612.

Miles & Directions

- 0.0 From Ridge Ave. and U.S. Hwy. 53 at the Galesville town square, proceed south on U.S. Hwy. 53.
- 0.3 Right on Harris Rd.
- 0.4 Left on Houston St. at the bottom of a short, steep hill.
- 0.7 At U.S. Hwy. 53 and Hwy. 54/93 proceed straight across and immediately turn right on Mckeeth Rd.
- 1.8 Right on Cooper Rd.
- 3.0 Right on McGilavary Rd.
- 3.9 Straight across County M onto Cox Rd.
- 4.6 Straight across County K.
- 6.7 Right on Schubert Rd.
- 8.2 Right on Hwy. 54/93. **Use caution, and ride on the paved shoulder because there may be considerable traffic.**
- 8.4 Left on Little Tamarack Rd.
- 9.3 Straight onto Hammond Rd.
- 10.5 Bear right on Sacia Rd.
- 13.9 Left on County T, if you're riding the long option.

To complete the shorter, 15.3-mile option, proceed straight onto County T, which becomes 4th St. in Galesville. At mile 14.7 turn left at W. Ridge Ave. At mile 15.3 you'll be back at the town square.

- 19.1 Veer to the right onto the short connector road past the B&D Fraust Implement Co. to U.S. Hwy. 53. This handful of buildings is Frenchville, and you'll find a soft drink machine at the gas station.
- 19.2 Right on U.S. Hwy. 53. **Caution: traffic.**
- 19.5 Left on Dopp Rd., which becomes Westle Rd.
- 24.0 Straight onto County D.
- 24.4 Proceed straight on County C at the intersection of County C and County D in the town of Ettrick, where you'll find a cafe and a convenience store.
- 26.7 At U.S. Hwy. 53 go straight across onto Kittleson Rd.
- 29.0 Left at County I.
- 32.3 Right onto County T at the intersection with County D.

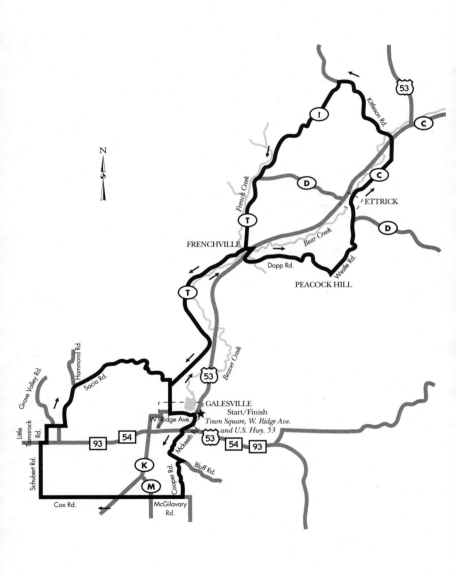

- 34.6 Stay right on County T at the junction with the short connector road to U.S. Hwy. 53 at Frenchville.
- 40.6 Left at W. Ridge Ave.
- 41.2 Arrive at the Galesville town square.

43

Nicolet Wheel-Away Cruise

The name Three Lakes is a bit of a misnomer, or at least an under-estimate. There are twenty-eight connected lakes in the area, making this the largest freshwater inland chain of lakes in the world. The lakes are musky country. Deep, clear waters hide the muskellunge, the fisherman's prize, a monster fish that can reach a length of 5 feet and a weight of nearly seventy pounds. But it's the lure of the surrounding Nicolet National Forest that attracts bicyclists to the annual Nicolet Wheel-Away, held on the Saturday of Labor Day Weekend.

You'll enjoy this ride most on a mountain bike or hybrid with somewhat fatter tires because there are several gravel roads. The route penetrates the heart of the forest, where deer and black bear are often seen. On your way from Three Lakes, you'll skirt the shore of Spirit Lake. Keep an eye open for a soaring bald eagle as you pass by this or any other open body of water. Eagles are great fishers. The sight of one dropping from the sky with its wings tucked in and suddenly unfurling them as it plucks an unlucky fish from the water is unforgettable.

As you enter the national forest, you'll roll through a close canopy of mixed hard and soft woods such as maple, yellow birch, pine, and spruce. Soon you'll be skirting the edge of the Headwaters Wilderness, the largest wilderness area in Wisconsin. It's on the right side along Forest Roads 2182 and 2176. You can compare the wild forest with the managed forest on the left. Periodic interpretive signs explain the methods of forest management.

On your ride through the woods, you'll pass the sites of several abandoned Civilian Conservation Corps (CCC) camps. All that's left today are a few old foundations, but between 1933 and World War II there were more than 300 camps, housing 400,000 men, all over the country. The camps provided work for unemployed young men during the depths of the Great Depression and, in turn, developed national and state parks and forests.

Most of the forests of northern Wisconsin had been logged around the turn of the century. Since most logging was done in the winter, when lakes, streams, and marshes were frozen, no real physical improvements were made. The loggers left a cut-over landscape, covered with slash, stumps, and brush, that was inaccessible and prone to forest fires. The CCC took on the task of fire suppression and trail, road, and bridge building, opening the forest to the public.

You may want to take a break at the boat landing on Butternut Lake, along Forest Road 2179. It's a popular spot for picnicking and enjoying the view. Farther along Butternut Road you'll pass stands of older-growth pine, hemlock, and maple before turning on Forest Road 2178. The road was the first to cut through this vast forest when it was built during the Civil War to connect Fort Howard at Green Bay with Fort Wilkins on Lake Superior. The threat of England and Canada coming into the war on the side of the Confederacy was real enough for the government to build a supply road, since the water route via the Great Lakes might have been in jeopardy. As it turned out, the road was unnecessary and few soldiers used it. A ride along it is as quiet and scenic today as it was then.

The Basics

Start: Park at the Three Lakes Recreation Park, 2 blocks west of U.S. Hwy. 45 on County A in Three Lakes.

Length: 48.4 miles.

Terrain: Rolling.

Food: There are several restaurants, a grocery, and a bakery in Three Lakes; otherwise there are no services on the route.

For more information: Nicolet Wheel-Away, Nicolet National Forest, 68 S. Stevens St., Rhinelander, WI 54501; (715) 362–1373. Three Lakes Information Bureau, P.O. Box 268, Three Lakes, WI 54562; (800) 972–6103.

Bicycle service: In nearby Eagle River.

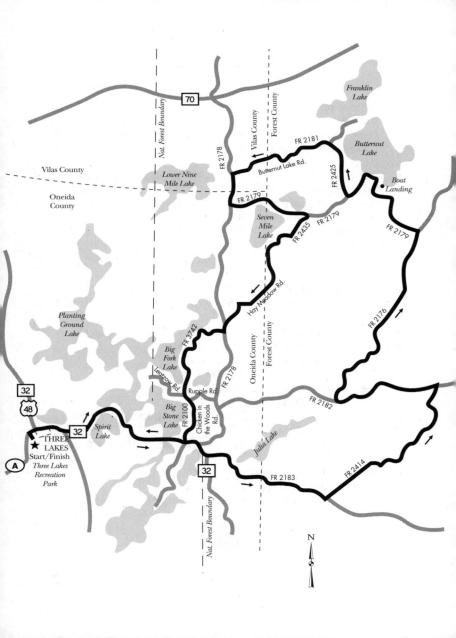

Miles & Directions

- 0.0 Proceed north from the parking lot of the Three Lakes Recreation Park.
- 0.2 Right on County A.
- 0.4 Proceed straight onto U.S. Hwy. 45 in the town of Three Lakes, where you'll find several restaurants, a grocery, and a bakery.
- 1.2 Bear left onto Hwy. 32. **Caution: Significant traffic may be encountered.**
- 5.9 Left on Forest Rd. 2183 (will be gravel for the last mile).
- 9.6 Left on Forest Rd. 2414 (gravel).
- 14.4 Left on Forest Rd. 2182 (Sheltered Valley Rd.).
- 17.3 Right on Forest Rd. 2176.
- 22.9 Left on Forest Rd. 2179 (gravel to the Butternut Lake boat landing).
- 26.3 Right on Forest Rd. 2425.
- 27.9 Left on Forest Rd. 2181, which becomes Butternut Lake Rd.
- 31.0 Left on Forest Rd. 2178 (Military Rd.)
- 31.9 Left on Forest Rd. 2179 (Knapp Rd.).
- 34.0 Right on Forest Rd. 2435.
- 37.0 Straight onto Forest Rd. 2178.
- 38.4 Right on Forest Rd. 3742.
- 41.5 Left on Leatzow Rd.
- 41.7 Right on Forest Rd. 2100 (Chicken in the Woods Rd.).
- 43.1 Right on Hwy. 32.
- 47.1 Straight onto Hwy. 32/U.S. Hwy. 45 in the town of Three Lakes.
- 48.0 Straight onto County A.
- 48.2 Left into Three Lakes Recreation Park.
- 48.4 Arrive at parking lot.

44

Chippewa Valley Cruise

The city of Chippewa Falls lies just a few miles south of the forty-fifth parallel of latitude. That puts it halfway between the Equator and the North Pole. It's a transition zone that marks the change from the scenic farmland to the vast woodlands that characterize Wisconsin. This tour, held annually on the Sunday of Memorial Day Weekend, spans the boundary area. In addition to the loop shown here, the tour includes 30-, 75-, and 100-mile routes. The postrace picnic features typical Wisconsin fare: bratwurst, Chippewa spring water, and Leinenkugel's beer.

The Leinenkugel brewery is near the southern entrance to Irvine Park. It's one of the few surviving small breweries in the Midwest. Tours and sampling are available on weekdays during the summer months by reservation at this picturesque brewery that dates back to 1867. German settlers like Jacob Leinenkugel brought the brewing skill to this country, and hundreds of small-town breweries thrived until Prohibition and, later, cutthroat competition from the big breweries put them under. Ironically, Leinenkugel's is now owned by the nation's second largest brewery, Miller of Milwaukee. Miller's ownership hasn't changed the Leinie's tradition of brewing fine beer with the spring water that the town claims is the purest in the world.

As you roll east and north from Chippewa Falls and cross the Chippewa River where it enters the flowage known as Lake Wissota, you'll pass the apple orchards and farms that prosper in spite of the diminished sunlight that marks the forty-fifth parallel. At Jim Falls you'll cross the Chippewa again at the site of one of the Midwest's state-of-the-art hydroelectric power plants.

For the next 10 miles, the road closely follows a wild and scenic stretch of the Chippewa. The river was once known as the Road of

War, and this area was a no-man's-land in the perennial conflict between the Ojibwa (Chippewa) and the Dakota (Sioux). The river was a direct route between the Madeline Island base of the Ojibwa on Lake Superior and the Red Wing base of the Dakota on the Mississippi. Battles in the Chippewa Valley occurred as late as 1854.

When logging began in the Chippewa Valley in 1838, more than one-sixth of the nation's white pine stood in its watershed. They were magnificent trees, 5 feet in diameter and 160 feet in height. The first white man to come to the area, English explorer Jonathan Carver, remarked on the towering trees on his journey up the Chippewa River in 1767.

The white pine isn't called "the tree that built America" for nothing, and in ninety years logging in the valley was over. By that time the mills were taking 5-inch logs. The great white pines were long gone. More than 60 percent had been wasted as stumps, slash, or sawdust or had been consumed by fire. Replanting began in 1920, and today the valley is your introduction to the picturesque white paper birch and pines that beautify the northern Wisconsin forest.

The Basics

Start: Park in Irvine Park, on the north side of Chippewa Falls, and begin riding in front of the Lower Park Pavilion.
Length: 59.8 miles.
Terrain: Rolling.
Food: There are many options in Chippewa Falls. There are a restaurant in Jim Falls and three supper clubs along Hwy. 178 north of town. You can detour off the route by following Hwy. 64 into Cornell, where you'll find a grocery, convenience stores, and restaurants. There is nowhere to get food on the second half of the route.
For more information: Kiwanis Chippewa Valley Century Ride & Run, 1037 Olive St., Chippewa Falls, WI 54729; (715) 723–6661. Jacob Leinenkugel Brewing Co., 1–3 Jefferson Ave., Chippewa Falls, WI 54729; (714) 723–5557.
Bicycle service: In Chippewa Falls.

Miles & Directions

- 0.0 From the Lower Park Pavilion, ride north on Irvine Park Dr.
- 0.4 Left at the GLEN LOCK sign.
- 0.7 Right at the SCENIC RD. sign and gate.
- 1.7 Right on County S at the north park entrance. **Caution: Significant traffic may be encountered during rush hours.**
- 2.5 Straight across Hwy. 124 onto County S.
- 3.5 Straight across Hwy. 178 onto County S.
- 5.8 Right on County O.
- 8.6 Left at Konerik Rd.
- 9.6 Right on Rollins Rd.
- 10.5 Left on Oak Ridge Dr.
- 14.1 Left on Clark St. in the village of Jim Falls, where you'll find a restaurant.
- 14.2 Right on E. 2nd St.
- 14.3 Right on N. Omaha St.
- 14.4 Proceed north on County Y (Main St.).
- 14.6 Right on Hwy. 178. **Caution: The road is narrow and twisty.**
- 25.0 Straight onto Hwy. 64.
- 25.8 Left on County CC.
- 26.7 Left on County Z.
- 34.8 Left on County E.
- 35.2 Right on Hwy. 64.
- 36.3 Left on Cornell Lake Dr.
- 37.1 Left on Prince Rd.
- 38.1 Right on Boot Lake Rd.
- 40.2 Left on Old Abe Rd.
- 44.0 Right on Hwy. 178.
- 46.1 Right on Highland Dr.
- 48.3 Straight across Hwy. 124.
- 49.2 Straight on O'Neil Creek Rd.
- 50.2 Left on Foker Rd.
- 50.7 Left on Baier Rd.
- 51.6 Right on W. Prairie Dr.
- 54.4 Straight on County B (W. Prairie Dr.).

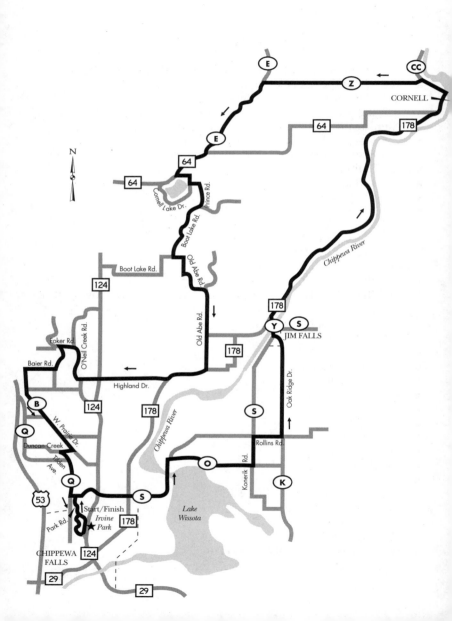

- 55.2 Straight on W. Prairie Dr. where County B bears left.
- 55.8 Right on Duncan Creek Rd.
- 56.3 Left on Tilden Ave.
- 56.6 Straight on County Q.
- 57.8 Left on County S. **Caution: Significant traffic may be encountered during rush hours.**
- 58.0 Right on Park Rd.
- 59.0 Right on Park Rd. at the T intersection.
- 59.2 Left at the Sunny Valley School.
- 59.8 Arrive at Lower Park Pavilion.

Appendix

The more you know, the more you can get out of the sport of bicycling. Not that it's rocket science, but various organizations and publications provide information, services, and camaraderie that add to the pleasure inherent in bicycling. National and local organizations act as sorting houses for information and work in the political arena to advocate changes that will benefit the bicycling community. Local clubs give the sport a social aspect, wielding clout on local bicycling issues and organizing frequent informal rides as well as the type of flagship tour on which most of the rides in this book are based. Regional magazines present timely cycling topics and up-to-date event calendars.

Bicycling Maps and Directories

Illinois Bicycle Maps & Bicycle Resources
Illinois Department of
    Transportation
Map Sales
2300 S. Dirkson Parkway
Springfield, IL 62764
(217) 782–0834
e-mail: http://www.dot.state.il.us
Free directory of available maps
and information.

Illinois Bicycling Guide
Illinois Department of Natural
    Resources
524 S. 2nd Street
Springfield, IL 62701-1787
(217) 782–7454; FAX (217)
    782–9552
e-mail: http://dnr.state.il.us
Free brochure listing rail-trail–
type bicycle facilities.

Indiana Ride Calendar
Indiana Bicycle Coalition
3649 Cold Spring Road
Indianapolis, IN 46222
(317) 327–8356; FAX (317)
    327–7224
Free listing of annual bicycle tours

Iowa Trail Guide
Iowa Natural Heritage Founda-
    tion
444 Insurance Exchange Building
505 5th Avenue
Des Moines, IA 50319
(515) 288–1846; (800) 345–IOWA
Free directory to rail-trail–type facilities.

Iowa's Recreation Trails
Iowa Department of
    Transportation
800 Lincoln Way
Ames, IA 50010
(515) 239–1621; FAX (515)
    239–1982

e-mail: nburns@iadot.e-mail.com
Free directory to rail-trail–type facilities.

Michigan Biking Information
Free brochure listing available bicycle maps and trail publications.

Bicycle Touring Michigan
Michigan Department of
    Transportation
Transportation Planning, Bike
    Information
P.O. Box 30050
Lansing, MI 48909
(517) 373–9815
e-mail: hixsonp@state.mi.us
Free brochure listing organized
bicycle tours.

Minnesota Bike Trail Packet
Minnesota DNR Information
    Center
500 Lafayette Road
St. Paul, MN 55155
(612) 269–6157; (800) 766–6000
Free packet of maps showing rail-trail–type bicycle facilities.

**Minnesota Quarter Section
Bicycle Maps**
$3.22 per section (plus $2.00
mailing charge no matter the
number of maps ordered). Each
section shows suitability ratings
of roads for bicycling in a quadrant of the state (northwest,
southwest, etc.).

Twin Cities Metro Bicycle Maps
$2.14 per section (plus $2.00
mailing charge no matter the
number of maps ordered). East
and west sections are available for
the Minneapolis/St. Paul Metro
areas showing suitability ratings
for bicycling on roads and streets.

Minnesota Department of
    Transportation
Map Sales, Mail Stop 260
395 John Ireland Boulevard
St. Paul, MN 55155
(make checks to MN DOT)

Ohio Bicycle Events Calendar
Free listing of annual bicycle
tours.

Bike Miami Valley Magazine
Miami Regional Bicycle Council
40 W. 4th Street, Suite 400
Dayton, OH 45402
(937) 463–2707; FAX (937)
    223–9750
e-mail: bikecncl@erinet.com
60-page bike trip planning guide.

**Ohio County by County Trail
Directory**
Ohio Department of
    Transportation
Bike–Ped Office, Room 707
25 S. Front Street
Columbus, OH 43215
(614) 644–7095;

FAX (614) 752–6534
e-mail: stodd@odot.dot.ohio.gov
Free directory to rail-trail–type facilities.

Seven County Chicago Bicycling Map

Comprehensive sheet map showing on-street routes and designated trails in the Chicago metro
area; $6.95.

Chicagoland Bicycle Federation
417 Dearborn Street
Suite 1800
Chicago, IL 60605
(312) 42–PEDAL
e-mail: chibikefed@aol.com

Wisconsin Bicycling Event Booklet

Bicycle Federation of Wisconsin
P.O. Box 1224
104 King Street, Suite 204
Madison, WI 53701
(608) 251–4456; FAX (608)
    255–1764
e-mail: bfw@mailbag.com
Free annual calendar of bicycling
events.

Bicycle Tour Operators

Columbus Outdoor Pursuits
P.O. Box 14384
Columbus, OH 43214
(614) 447–0888; FAX (614)
    262–1001
e-mail: http://www.on2morn-
ing.com/cop/goba.html
**Great Ohio Bicycle Adventure
(GOBA).** A circular-route, seven-
day tour beginning on the third
Sunday of June, featuring luggage
transport, camping, showers, support van, and repair, first-aid, and
medical services.
**Tour of the Scioto River Valley
(TOSRV).** The granddaddy of all
American organized tours, now in
its fourth decade, features a two-
day run on Mother's Day weekend in the Scioto River Valley
with luggage transport, camping,
meals, support van, and repair,
first-aid, and medical services.

Des Moines Register
P.O. Box 622
Des Moines, IA 50303-0622
(800) 532–1455, ext. 8285; FAX
    (515) 284–8138
e-mail: hucg96a@prodigy.com
**Register's Annual Great Bicycle
Ride Across IOWA (RAGBRAI).**
A seven-day point-to-point tour
beginning Sunday of the last full
week of July. Applications available January 1; must be received

by April 1. Tour features luggage transport, camping, showers, support vans, and repair, first-aid, and medical services.

GRABAAW
P.O. Box 310
Spring Green, WI 53588
(608) 935–RIDE
Great Annual Bicycle Adventure Along the Wisconsin River (GRABAAW). A week-long, late-June tour that traces the Wisconsin River from its headwaters to the confluence with the Mississippi, featuring luggage transport, camping, meals, support van, and repair and first-aid services.

Joliet Bicycle Club
2704 W. Dove Drive
Channohon, IL 60410
(815) 476–2044
Across Illinois Bike Ride (AIBR)
A four-day, early-August, 300-mile route from Moline on the Mississippi to New Lennox, including luggage transport, camping, four meals, support van, and repair and first-aid services.

Michigan Bicycle Touring
3512 Red School Road
Ingsley, MI 49649
(616) 263–5885; FAX (616) 263–7885
e-mail: bikembt@traverse.com

A commercial tour operator with over twenty years of experience offering a season-length calendar of two- to five-day bike tours, bike & hike tours, bike & canoe tours, and bike maintenance workshops for road and mountain bikes in the upper and lower peninsulas of Michigan and parts of Wisconsin and Indiana. Tours feature lodging at inns, bed & breakfasts, and resorts, support vans, and other services.

Minnesota MS Society
2344 Nicollet Avenue, #280
Minneapolis, MN 55404-3381
(612) 870–1500; (800) 582–5296
The Ride Across Minnesota (TRAM). A 300-mile, six-day, pledge-based, late-July tour featuring luggage transport, camping, entertainment, support van and repair, and first-aid services.

Out Spokin' Adventures
409 N. Court Street
Sparta, WI 54656
(608) 269–6087; (800) 4–WEBIKE
A commercial operator with over six years of experience offering one- to nine-day tours in Illinois, Iowa, Wisconsin, and Minnesota. Tours feature camping, inns, hotels, bed & breakfasts, support van, guides, equipment rental, vegetarian meals, all meals, or breakfast & dinner only.

Powwow Bicycle Tours
c/o Dennis & Peggy Northey
3533 W. Lapham Street
Milwaukee, WI 53215
(414) 671–4560
A commercial operator with over ten years of experience offering three tours per year from two to six days in length in Wisconsin. Tours include luggage transport, support van, college dorm lodging, vegetarian meals, breakfast & dinner only.

Wheel & Sprocket
6955 N. Port Washington Road
Glendale, WI 53217
(800) 362–4537
Sprocket's Annual Great Bike Ride Across Wisconsin (SAG-BRAW). An early August, multi-day tour that begins at various locations and ends in Milwaukee, featuring luggage transport, camping, meals, support van, and repair, first-aid, and medical services.

Bicycling Organizations

Adventure Cycling
P.O. Box 8308
Missoula, MT 59807
(406) 721–1776
Conducts tours, produces maps, and furnishes information on bicycle touring including the *Cyclist's Yellow Pages*, a state-by-state resource of information contacts.

Bicycle Federation of America
(BFA)
1506 21st Street NW
Suite 200
Washington, DC 20036
(202) 463–6622
Disseminates information on all aspects of cycling through a monthly newsletter and other publications. The BFA conducts research on topics affecting bicycling and holds a biennial conference.

Bicycle Federation of Wisconsin
104 King Street
Suite 204
Madison, WI 53701-1224
(608) 251–4456
Promotes recreational and transportation bicycling as well as access, safety, and other issues.

Chicagoland Bicycle Federation
417 Dearborn Street
Suite 1800
Chicago, IL 60605
(312) 427–3325
Represents the interests of cyclists in the Chicago metro area and publishes an excellent bicycle route map.

Hostelling International AYH
P.O. Box 37613
Washington, DC 20013-7613
(202) 783–6161
A system of 150 hostels provides inexpensive lodging for bicyclists. Hostelling Inernational AYH is affiliated with more than thirty regional clubs that offer organized bike tours.

League of American Bicyclists (LAB)
190 W. Ostend Street
Suite 120
Baltimore, MD 21230
(410) 539–3399
The LAB is the parent organization for a great many touring clubs in the U.S. It is the most active organization in lobbying for bicyclists' rights and needs on both state and national levels. Membership includes a subscription to the magazine *Bicycle USA*.

The Ohio Bicycle Federation
P.O. Box 15060
Cleveland, OH 44115
Ohio has a very extensive bicycle club system that organizes more than seventy tours annually. Send a S.A.S.E. for information on weekend bicycle tours in the state.

Rails-to-Trails Conservancy
1400 16th Street NW
Washington, DC 20036
(202) 797–5400
Advocates utilizing abandoned railroad right-of-ways for the purpose of self-propelled recreation.

U.S.A. Cycling, Inc.
One Olympia Plaza
Colorado Springs, CO 80909
(719) 578–4581
Represents amateur and professional bicycle racing in the United States.

Regional Sports Magazines

Michigan Cyclist
Castelli Publications
150 Fountain NE
Grand Rapids, MI 49503
(616) 454–0155
A free quarterly tabloid devoted to bicycling in Michigan, with feature articles and a calendar of events.

Midwest Bike
1350 W. 5th Avenue
Suite 30
Columbus, OH 43212
(614) 486–2202
A free tabloid published nine
times a year, featuring an extensive calendar listing and covering
bicycling events in Ohio, Indiana,
and the southern peninsula of
Michigan.

Minnesota Sports
Skyway Publications Inc.
15 S. Fifth Street
Suite 800
Minneapolis, MN 55402
(612) 375–9045
A free monthly tabloid featuring
articles and an events calendar
covering bicycling and other
sports in Minnesota in general
and the Twin Cities metro area in
particular.

Silent Sports
P.O. Box 152
Waupaca, WI 54981
(715) 258–5546
A subscription-based monthly
magazine covering bicycling and
other sports in Wisconsin, Minnesota, northern Illinois, Iowa,
and Michigan. Each issue includes a very complete calendar
of events.

Windy City Sports
Windy City Publishing
1450 W. Randolph
Chicago, IL 60607
(312) 421–1551
A free monthly tabloid featuring
articles and a calendar of events
related to bicycling and other
sports in the Chicago metro area
and beyond.

Tourism Offices

These state offices will send general tourism information and, in
some cases, specific material on
bicycling.

Illinois Bureau of Tourism
Travel Information Center
310 S. Michigan Avenue
Suite 108
Chicago, IL 60604
(312) 814–4732

Indiana Division of Tourism,
     Dept. of Commerce
One N. Capitol Avenue
Suite 700
Indianapolis, IN 46204-2288
(317) 232–8860

Iowa Department of Economic
Development
Division of Tourism
200 E. Grand
Des Moines, IA 50309
(515) 242–4705

Travel Bureau
Michigan Department of
Commerce
P.O. Box 30226
Lansing, MI 48909
(800) 5432–YES

Minnesota Office of Tourism
100 Metro Square
121 7th Place E
St. Paul, MA 55101-2112
(800) 657–3700
296–5029 (in metro area)

Ohio Division of Travel and
Tourism
P.O. Box 1001
Columbus, OH 43266-0101
(800) BUCKEYE

Wisconsin Department of
Tourism
P.O. Box 7976
Madison, WI 53707-7976
(800) 432–8747
Request the *Wisconsin Biking
Guide.*

About the Author

Phil Van Valkenberg has been a cyclist for thirty of his fifty-two years. Durin_ that time he has organized numerous bicycling events in his native Wisc_ sin. He has written several bicycle touring books for the state and was respo sible for producing the official state bicycle map.

Acknowledgments

No project of this magnitude can be the result of only one person's effort. It would not have been possible without the response and support of a great number of people. In particular, I'd like to thank Tom Conway of the Bicyclists of Iowa City; Jeff Stegemeyer of the Galesville Apple Affair Bike Tour; Arland Cutler of the Muskegon Bicycle Club; Sean Morris and Randy Neufeld of the Chicagoland Bicycle Federation; Brian Volstorf, organizer of the Apple Cider Century; Dan McKay, director of Another Dam Bike Ride; Neil Bard at the Richland Medical Center; Bill Kelleher of the Akron Bicycle Club; Gene Van Alstine of the Rum River Bicycle Classic; Mary Clark of the Big River Bicycle Club; and David Peterson and Jay and Donna DeNovo of the Bombay Bicycle Club.

I'd also like to thank the following contributors: Mark Garlikov of the Dayton Cycling Club; Don Hertzler, organizer of the Crossroads Bike Tour; Brian Sittler, director of the Covered Bridge Century; Kathy LaPlante of the Chippewa Valley Century; Carol Rose at the Child Guidance Center in Traverse City, Michigan; Kevin Vachow of the Big Mac Scenic Shoreline Tour; Tim Castelli of the Blackhawk Bicycle and Ski Club; John Gardner of the Michiana Bicycle Association; Cindy Steinbach of the Audubon Days Bike Tour; Joe Anderson of the Bloomington Bicycle Club; David Schultz of the Medina County Bicycle Club; Jeff Stephens of the American Lung Association of Michigan; Ron Gonterman of the Licking County Bicycle Club; Paul Hansen of the Toledo Council American Youth Hostels; Bruce Dalman of the North Country Century Ride; Mark Lennon of the Velo Duluth Cycle Club; Phil Barker at the Nicolet National Forest; Diane Baumann at the Park Rapids Chamber of Commerce; Sheryl Hansen and Steve Shaffer of the Illinois Valley Wheelmen; Roger Kalter of the Marietta Rowing and Cycle Club; Julie and Tom Morneau of the Thumbs Up Bicycle Club; Suzie LaForce of the Quad Cities Bicycle Club; and Lynn Hodson and Charley Myer of the Wabash River Bicycle Club.

Many thanks to my editors and all of the other people who encouraged me in this project; to those who offered insights and advice that have made this a great collection of tours; and to the bicycle tourists of America, who have changed the character of outdoor recreation over the past twenty-five years.